patch, MIR Campaign 2003

Morag Wightman, Falling without Fear, 2001
Photo: GCTC/The Arts Catalyst

ZER0GRAVITY
невесомость

A Cultural User's Guide

The Arts Catalyst

Edited by Nicola Triscott & Rob La Frenais

Published by The Arts Catalyst
www.artscatalyst.org

Copyright © 2005
The Arts Catalyst, the authors

ISBN 0-9534546-4-9

All rights reserved. Except for the quotation of short passages for the purposes of criticism and review, no part of this publication may be reproduced, stored in a retrieval system or transmitted, in any form or by any means, without the prior permission of the publisher and authors.

Photography credited within publication.

Every attempt has been made to trace the copyright holders of the images in this book. Any missing credits brought to our attention will be rectified in future impressions.

Designed and printed with support from the European Commission Culture 2000 Fund and the Arts Council of England

Edited by Nicola Triscott
and Rob La Frenais
Publication coordinated by Miranda Pope
Project Manager Gillean Dickie
Designed at PKMB
Printed in Belgium by Snoeck-Ducaju & Zoon

06 Introduction, Nicola Triscott

Essays

08 *An Introduction to Vertigo*, Rob La Frenais
11 *Once Upon a Space Age*, Marina Benjamin
14 *Being There*, Mikhail Ryklin
18 *Against Gravitropism: Art and the Joys of Levitation*, Eduardo Kac
26 *Achieving Levity*, Judith Palmer
28 *On the Use and Abuse of Microgravity for Life*, Kodwo Eshun

32 Projekt Atol Flight Operations, Marko Peljhan
38 A Partial History of Parabolic Flight (& of feeling sick), Louise K Wilson

Projects

46 Kitsou Dubois
52 Mike Stubbs
54 Ansuman Biswas & Jem Finer
60 Andrew Kötting
62 Morag Wightman
66 Anthony Bull, Louise K Wilson, Morag Wightman
68 Flow Motion – Edward George, Anne Piva, Trevor Mattison
70 Andrey & Julia Velikanov
72 Nick Davey & team: Imperial College Biodynamics Group / Ki Productions / The Arts Catalyst
74 Marcel.li Antúnez Roca
78 Yuri Leiderman
80 Otolith Group – Kodwo Eshun, Anjalika Sagar, Richard Couzins
82 Vadim Fishkin
84 i-DAT
86 Stefan Gec
88 Rebecca Forth
90 Ewen Chardronnet

92 Participants on Arts Catalyst flights / expeditions

94 Contributors

95 Thanks. Credits

Star City, Russia
Photo: The Arts Catalyst

Introduction

Nicola Triscott

Listening to Sean O'Keefe, current head of NASA, promoting George Bush and NASA's new vision of manned Mars missions at the 55th International Astronautical Congress in October 2004 (1), you could have gained the impression that the entire focus of space exploration over the past 50 years and for the future has been a unilateral devotion to one goal: to put Americans (and its fluctuating allies, now including the Russians) on the various planets of the solar system, starting with the moon, next step Mars. "This is" announced blockbuster film-maker and NASA advisor James Cameron, "what the public wants!"

Even within the space community, this vision is highly contentious. Outside that small world, it attempts to convey an anaesthetised Hollywood vision rather than dealing with the complex and global nature of interests in space: political, military, economic, scientific, technical and cultural. Prior to this retro-revival of the old Space Dream, space agency PR was an increasingly unconvincing and tired argument for scientific benefits and technology spin-offs.

It is time to develop and realise an alternative vision of space exploration for a new global space age. A vision that understands that space is not just the preserve of NASA and the West but is rooted historically in cultures across the globe. One that perceives that space is not a territory "out there" waiting to be conquered or simply a resource for the transfer of techno-science benefits. Paradoxically, the Arts Catalyst started its search in Star City, heart of the Russian space programme, where the philosophical and artistic idealism of Russian cosmism, dreamed up 100 years ago, still permeate its present day space efforts..

This book is being published both as a 'cultural users guide' to zero gravity and to mark six years of work by the UK-based science-art agency, The Arts Catalyst, with its several partners, in particular the Slovenian Projekt Atol Flight Operations and the European MIR network (2), in enabling artists and scientists to access zero gravity conditions on parabolic flights and related space facilities. It provides a historical record of the projects that have emerged and attempts to describe the various contexts for this work.

To defy gravity is to defy the accepted, the unquestioned and the status quo. It is to embrace the unknown and to map a new territory, personal, artistic and political. The MIR programme – the wider context of Arts Catalyst's space activities, a group of international arts organisations promoting cultural engagement with space – is fundamentally a way of inviting wider reflection and dialogue on the state of the world. It uses independent artistic, scientific and cultural experiments to call for democratisation of space, a rethinking of current operational models and peaceful use of space technologies. Such work rests within a contemporary artistic and scientific interest in interdisciplinarity. It is increasingly understood that a repositioning or reconnecting of different specialised areas of investigation is necessary for an outward-looking, innovative and ethical society. This book asks that imagination be used to connect research to wider society and culture and envisage the implications.

My colleague Rob La Frenais in his "Introduction to Vertigo" recalls his first zero gravity flight in Star City, Russia, at the invitation of our now long-time collaborator Marko Peljhan of Projekt Atol, and conveys how this all started. He also attempts to address the gap between a popular imaginary of weightlessness and its reality.

Marina Benjamin sketches a new understanding of the real cultural legacy of the Apollo programme. Enchanted, as 60s children were, by Apollo, she still idealises the astronauts, only now because of an achievement that time has enabled us to understand, that they "snatched the moon landings away from the Cold War myth mongers who orchestrated them and redefined them as the moment that permitted humankind to take stock of itself." By going into space, Benjamin contends, we discovered the Earth. She too suggests we now need a "new mythos" for space.

Russian philosopher Mikhail Ryklin also reflects on his first experience of weightlessness. His task more elusive than most we have taken into parabolic flight, simply to reflect on his own state during the different phases of the zero gravity flight. With the knowledge of one who has worked to reconcile the old ideals of Russian cosmism with the New Russia's free market, he also discusses the context of Star City for many of our flights.

Zero gravity art is naturally contextualised within the history of artistic avant-garde movements and we include an updated version of Eduardo Kac's essay 'Against Gravitropism', which maps a history of art in defiance of gravity, from Moholy-Nagy to future possibilities opened up by space tourism and electromagnetism.

Judith Palmer explains the difficulties of recreating conditions of weightlessness adequately on earth and the history of these attempts.

Kodwo Eshun calls for a critical inventory of art in parabolic flight, which he describes as "a peculiarly under-theorised sector of contemporary art practice". In the traditions of site-specific art, the work should invest the spaces it occupies with different or deeper meanings than their normal association. The artist must understand the physical and ideological properties of the space and use these to create art that could not otherwise be realised.

Marko Peljhan gives an account of the first theatre performance in parabolic flight organised by Projekt Atol and records the events leading to the founding of the MIR network.

To date, more than 20 artists have created artistic work in zero gravity environments. In the bizarre world of parabolic flight, the total accumulated time of all these artists' experiences in zero gravity is only a few hours at most. Roger Malina, astrophysicist and editor and chairman of Leonardo, The International Society for the Arts, Sciences and Technology, has expressed concern that art in zero gravity may, in the history of art, remain only as a footnote (3). In view of burgeoning opportunities for parabolic flight (4) and, on the horizon, private access to space heralded by SpaceShipOne – which in 2004 won the X prize for the first repeatable commercial space flight – the demise of cultural experiments in this domain seems unlikely. But seen in a broader context and for the individual artists, even if it were never to be repeated, it has value and, we hope, legacy.

(1) 55th International Astronautical Congress, Vancouver, Canada, 5 – 8 October 2004

(2) The MIR network comprises:

The Arts Catalyst, the science-art agency, London, UK
V2, Institute for the Unstable Media, Rotterdam, The Netherlands
Projekt Atol, Ljubljana, Slovenia
Leonardo/Olats, Paris, France & USA
Multimedia Complex for the Actual Arts, Moscow, Russia
SpaceArtOne, Paris, France

MIR stands for Microgravity Interdisciplinary Research and pays homage to the Russian Mir orbital space station, which was brought back down to Earth the day before the MIR network was founded.

(3) "Contextualizing Zero-Gravity Art" – Roger Malina, Leonardo Electronic Almanac volume 11, number 9, September 2003

(4) Such as the pay-per-person Star City flights with Space Adventures, Zero Gravity Arts Consortium in the States (www.zgac.org/index.htm), and Xero, based in Sweden

Ilyushin-76 MDK
Photo: Alex Adriaansens

An Introduction to Vertigo

Rob La Frenais

It's often been said that it is difficult to argue with the laws of physics at 30,000 feet. It is even more difficult to argue with them if the plane that you are in describes a perfect parabola, allowing you to experience 30 seconds of zero gravity sandwiched between two sections of double gravity, and then does it again and again, creating a notion of what it could be like if your body could, actually, fly. This experience, which has been undertaken by more and more non-astronauts, including recently, artists, over the past 40 years (in fact before Gagarin's flight) is the ultimate intersection between hard scientific reality and humanity's age-old fantasy, the dream of flight. The out-of body experience, the flying carpet, the flying broomstick, shamanic journey and yogic flying all collide with a metaphorical impact with the purely visceral flesh and blood experience of the human body, organs and all, being lifted out of the bonds of gravity.

To imagine leaving gravity behind it is necessary to do a little visualisation exercise. You are sitting in your chair reading this. You can not only feel the reassuring push of the chair against your bottom, your feet on the ground, but also in the way your arm rests on the table, your stomach positioned above the pelvis, the blood flowing in your veins and arteries gently weighing down on you, this book resting in your grasp. Now imagine all that departing in an instant. What a catastrophe it would be if gravity suddenly were to be cancelled out on Earth!

But it is possible to adapt? Long-staying cosmonauts and astronauts use little tricks to maintain their gravity-dependent selves, like strapping themselves into their sleeping bags so they can sleep with the sensation of the covers pressing down on them. They are constantly having to tie things down, using velcro and other products. They have ingenious uses for all three dimensions. They also learn that you can leave objects floating mid-air, but only for specific lengths of time. They swim around their space stations, Mir and now the International Space Station, but when they sit down for meals they all face each other the same way up to squirt food and liquids into their mouths. After only a week in zero gravity the re-adaptation to Earth gravity becomes a major problem. They have to work out continuously. The trip to Mars may be a one-way ticket unless we take gravity with us. All this is known.

The problem is that there is also a fundamental reality gap between the experiences of the community of 600 or so astronauts and cosmonauts, members of the exclusive club who have travelled into space, and the general public who live in normal gravity conditions. Some people even imagine that somewhere in NASA or a similar space training facility exists an anti-gravity room, where gravity can be switched off and people float around.

This doesn't exist, although in recent years, experiments in diamagnetism have allowed organic matter, even animals, though not yet humans, to be floated using a combination of strong magnets and the weak magnetic force existing in everything, the 'floating frog' being the best-known example. The Dutch Experiment Support Centre in Nimegen now offers this technique to scientists wishing to investigate the effects of varying gravity on living materials, in some cases in combination with the parabolic flight facilities offered by the European Space Agency. This is as close to an anti-gravity chamber as we have got, so, devoid of actual experience, the public only has mythology and literary metaphor to work with.

How different is the first zero gravity experience from a typical literary description? An evocative and intelligent recent example is to be found in Paul Auster's 'Mr Vertigo', where the young hero, Walter Rawley, is put through a number of depredations by the Hungarian showman Master Yehudi until 'There were no more tears to be gotten out of me – only a dry choked heaving, an aftermath of hiccups and scorched airless breaths. Presently I grew still, almost tranquil, and bit by bit a sense of calm spread through me, radiating out among my muscles and oozing toward the tips of my fingers and toes. There were no more thoughts in my head, no more feelings in my heart. I was weightless inside my own body, floating on a placid wave of nothingness, utterly detached and indifferent to the world around me. And that's when I did it for the first time – without warning, without the least notion that it was about to happen. Very slowly I felt my body rise off the floor. The movement was so natural, so exquisite in its gentleness, it wasn't until I opened my eyes that I understood my limbs were touching only air. I was not far off the ground – no more than an inch or two – but I hung there without effort, suspended like the moon in the night sky, motionless and aloft, conscious only of the air fluttering in and out of my lungs'.

An earlier example, significantly from Russian culture, both geographically the homeland of nomadic tribes legendarily harbouring reindeer-powered trance-induced flying shamen, and the actual birthplace of human spaceflight, is this description of 'flying cream' from Mikhail Bulgakov's classic 'The Master and Margarita': ...Margarita jumped out of her bathrobe with a single leap, dipped freely into the light, rich cream, and with vigorous strokes began rubbing it into the skin of her body. It at once turned pink and tingly. That instant, as if a needle had been snatched from her brain, the ache she had felt all evening in her temple subsided...her leg and arm muscles grew stronger and then Margarita's body became weightless. She sprang up and hung in the air just above the rug, then was slowly pulled down and descended. What a cream! What a cream! cried Margarita, throwing herself into an armchair.'

Interestingly there is little difference between these two descriptions, although the latter is written before many years before the first spaceflight and the former written after.

What are the other analogues to the zero gravity experience? Skydiving, circus acts, deep-sea diving all produce experiences that alter the effects of gravity in different ways, and all these have been used by artists approaching reduced gravity at different times. It is significant that the first person to approach space agencies with a view to turning the flying dream into reality, was the determined and highly motivated choreographer and dancer, Kitsou Dubois.

Influenced by Gaston Bachelard's statements in 'Air and Dreams' (among other texts) and inspired by a meeting with distinguished French astronaut Claudie Deshayes, Dubois set off on a one-woman mission to storm the defences of the carefully-guarded space establishment. Arriving at NASA's Goddard Space Centre, armed with an introduction, Dubois was nevertheless given short shrift by NASA. 'I was French, I was a dancer, I was a woman'. Undaunted, Dubois managed to get a foot in the door with the French Space agency, CNES and in 1993 boarded the Caravelle Zero Gravity plane to become the first professional artist to intentionally experience zero gravity.

Watching those first video records of Dubois' 'birth' into zero gravity (technically microgravity) is both haunting and instructive, as you see her initial joy at flying for the first time being slowly replaced by her putting into action her dance training in this new environment. The first moments of the zero G experience in a parabolic flight can for some, be both traumatic and revelatory. Putting aside the well-known side-effect of nausea, usually experienced after four or five parabolic sequences of weightlessness, there is an aspect of disorientation, in which all the senses are discombombulated, the inner ear loses control and you are forced, as the Russian instructors in Star City put it, to 'test your emotional stability'.

My own first experience of flying in the Russia Ilyushin-76 MDK craft back in 1999, six years after Dubois' first flight was not helped by a complete state of unpreparedness and a mild problem of vertigo. I had been called to Star City, the former secret cosmonaut training base, near Moscow with three days notice (Get visa! Get medical!) by Marko Peljhan, a friend and long-time collaborator, who had put together the project in a last minute firefight for the explosive and charismatic Slovenian theatre director Dragan Zhivadinov. Zhivadinov, who was later to mount the first full-scale theatre performance, complete with audience, on the Ilyushin, had earlier made a solo flight as part of a cigarette company-sponsored 'space training' competition the previous year in the new free-for all Russia, and Peljhan had had previous contact with the Russian space agency through the organisation of a live video conference with the Kristall mission on the Mir space station.

Arriving after a whirlwind of last-minute preparations we arrived at the gate of Star City in an aged 'cosmonaut bus'. We were clearly in unknown territory, waiting for over 3 hours to find someone in charge. A variety of officers in greatcoats and the characteristic Russian military big hats came back and forth with contradictory messages, but the Slovenian team, all Russian space buffs, kept spotting space legends entering and leaving. There's Leonov! And Krikalev!

I remember feeling a mixture of anxiety and disbelief that we would ever be allowed to actually take off, but in what seemed no time at all we were lined up like military recruits with parachutes, after an apparently cursory medical exam, and taking off in what appeared to be a rather creaky but enormous jet plane, smelling of oil, jet fuel and feeling as if I hadn't missed the second world war and conscription in my lifetime after all. To my bemusement and even further disbelief my trainer for the flight was none other than Yuri Gidzenko, another legendary long-duration Mir cosmonaut and later to command the mission to build the International Space Station. Sergei Krikalev (the Last Soviet Citizen, stranded on Mir during the fall of communism) also joined us for the ride.

The first moment of zero gravity is one of those 'wake-up' moments where you feel like you have been dreaming for the rest of your life. Nothing quite computes, you feel as if you are somehow a character in a strange movie. I felt a sharp tingling of the blood around my extremities, followed by a massive panic attack. Time to test my emotional stability. In one direction to the left of my field of vision flew one of the Slovenian actors, stage-diving, hair flying, laughing. Gidzenko hovered solicitously upside down near me – 'Are you OK?'. I nodded, stiff upper lip operational, as he flew off diagonally to play a game of 3 dimensional tag with Krikalev.

'It's the most expensive drug in the world' Zhivadinov said later, and seeing the cosmonauts get their fix, I could see why. Coming to terms with the effects of the drug myself, I could begin to see the disadvantages of my lack of preparedness. I could, for example have taken part in one of the training courses in movement in microgravity Kitsou Dubois now gives in warm swimming pools. Instead, I controlled myself with deep breathing and performed an approximate yogic flying posture for two parabolas. Later I even tried to fly. Peljhan said afterwards it looked like the first attempt by anyone to crawl in zero gravity.

Coming to the ground, despite feeling as if I had either overdosed or escaped a fatal road accident, and having survived the traditional post-flight vodka toast, it became apparent however that this was a procedure that most healthy people could undertake. My colleague in the Arts Catalyst, Nicola Triscott, for example, took to zero gravity like a duck to water in the first flight we organised on realising it was possible to work in Star City. This marked the start of the first sustained zero gravity programme for artists in the world. Since then, in the last 5 years the Arts Catalyst has enabled 50 people to experience microgravity, undertaken over 14 artists projects, 3 scientific projects, a radio broadcast, a short science-fiction film and flown a robot.

Mykhail Rylin later describes well the atmosphere at Star City, a sixties Soviet time capsule, haunted by the ghosts of Gagarin and blown by the winds of Russian cosmist philosophy. We too haunted this place for four years, discovering its peculiarities and difficulties to allow the largest group of artistically-minded civilians ever to penetrate the secret world of cosmonaut training.

As a result of the Arts Catalyst expeditions the reality gap between the public perception of flying the human body and the private world of the astronauts and cosmonauts has been closed a little. There are however whole areas of space flight training that remain closed to artists, or any one else for that matter. The next step is to get the European Space Agency, for example, to take seriously the idea of involving artists and writers in operational scenarios, in training and eventually into space, if the commercial sector does not get there first.

In preparation for this the next area of interest could be Mars gravity, partial gravity, or even double gravity. The use of the centrifuge as a space flight simulator has yet to be explored, although a non-human art project (see Stefan Gec) has been organised in the Star City programme. Again, artists are also getting interested in diamagnetism. If you can float a frog, what else can you float?

We may not have 'flying cream' or antigravity chambers yet, but the chance of exploring different gravities with a view to exploring open space is now a reality for artists who might be inclined to follow that path. But first there are some hurdles to cross.

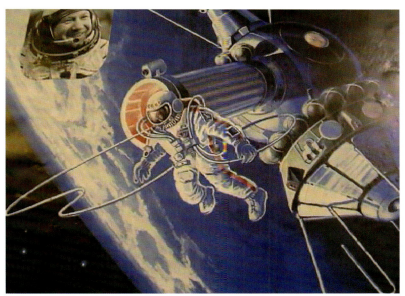

Painting in Star City
Image: Gagarin Cosmonaut Training Centre (GCTC)

Once Upon A Space Age

Marina Benjamin

The wildlands of northern Michigan, in America's Midwest, are a wonderful place to witness atmospheric phenomena. Without urban glare or highway lighting to interfere with nature's own illuminations every celestial sideshow can take centre stage.

This summer I was lucky enough to see a distorted moon over Bear Lake, magnified a hundred fold by water droplets in the air. Such a vision is increasingly hard to come by on our ever-developing planet and it held particular joy for me. Though it's been more than thirty years since a human bounced across the lunar surface, I still find myself virtually unable to look at the moon without seeing it as a destination, and sometimes, when my mind takes imaginative flight, as a possible alternative home. Enlarged as it was in the summer sky, that night the moon seemed enticingly proximate.

The setting was perfect. A group of us was gathered round a camp fire, with the lake in front of us, where a few tethered row boats quietly bobbed, and behind us was woodland that ringed the lake and stretched away into the rural wilderness. Hanging low and heavy in the darkening sky, the moon looked like an oversized paper lantern, luminous and orange as the setting sun, and it appeared to be floating just above the trees tops. The adults present oohed and aahed at the beauty of the spectacle and craned their necks back to get a better view. But the children quickly got bored. "Let's go chase fireflies," said one of them. "Who cares about the moon?"

I recognized that night, once again, that my unfashionable affection for the moon dates me. It marks me out as a child of the Space Age, doomed to disappointment because we never made it past Luna's first base to Mars and beyond. It dates me as someone who remembers that space was once imbued with transcendental import and that exploring its inky depths was allowed to stand for all that was best in humanity: bravery, expansiveness, curiosity, and ingenuity. It also dates me because it sets me apart from a younger generation that sees space, when it bothers to look, as the means through which it gets MTV, and that thinks of astronauts as little more than high-priced mechanics who whiz into the skies to plant satellites in orbit or fix telescopes.

To me, astronauts were always heroic figures. Back in those days I admired them simply for having made it to an alien world. What a surreal achievement! But in retrospect, I honour them for having snatched the moon landings away from the Cold War myth mongers who orchestrated them and redefined them as the moment that permitted humankind to take stock of itself.

Like millions of people born in the sixties, I was in thrall to the Apollo program and I grew up believing that floating space colonies, missions to Mars and intergalactic joyrides would be predictable milestones of my adult life, like learning to drive a car or becoming a mother. What I was no doubt picking up on was the conviction that technology would somehow transform the human condition – a conviction that permeated culture at large, thanks to the fact that space science seemed for a while at least to be keeping pace with the science fiction futures predicted by writers such as Isaac Asimov and Arthur C. Clarke. The message such writers conveyed was that space exploration was as natural to us as, in the words Buckminster Fuller, "a child running around on its own legs". In short, today we would conquer the moon, tomorrow we'd seize Mars and before long the whole galactic treasure trove would be ours for the taking.

By the time Stanley Kubrick's 2001: A Space Odyssey hit cinema screens in 1968, few people thought to question the now famous scene where, via a deft match cut, a bone club hurled into the air by primitive man morphs poetically into the arm of a rotating space station. Mankind's future in space, Kubrick seemed to be implying, was not a contingent path of human development, one of many. Space was pre-figured in the very birth of technology.

The trouble is that, poetics aside, technology could not ultimately fulfill the Space Age's air-whipped fantasies of cosmic conquest: that we never got beyond the moon, for example, represents a feeble effort by cosmic standards – equivalent to skipping stones across a backyard puddle. Part of the problem is that the visionary scientists who initially drove the space program both in America and the Soviet Union were forced to take a back seat to bureaucratic pragmatists who understood how to prolong the survival of their respective space agencies in a climate of ever-diminishing resources. But even the visionaries could not sidestep the conceptual difficulties posed by the fact that the distances involved in space travel are simply too great for the old Age of Exploration metaphors to work. It's the problem of seeing the moon as a kind of Ascension Island, midway between human colonies that might someday trade with one another.

In addition, it quickly became clear that human bodies are not well suited to long-haul space travel. Even relatively short stays in space can produce profound changes in the body, consistent with what NASA euphemistically terms "space adaptation syndrome": a loss of red blood cells, a reduced ability to exercise, a diminishment of bone density, weight loss, cardiac arrhythmia, evening a lengthening of the body. It's almost as if experience's answer to the space pundits' urgings that we venture boldly into the cosmic unknown is to suggest that going into space entails some kind of trespass, or evolutionary crime. At the very least, there is a real physical price to pay for travelling in space.

Even before the Apollo program fell to Earth, we had already managed to internalise much of the Space Age's outward-bound rhetoric. When, a short while back, I asked Apollo 12 astronaut Dick Gordon what we achieved by going to the moon, he told me, "We discovered the Earth". Virtually all the astronauts of Apollo were overcome by extraordinary homesickness as they found themselves circling Luna's alien sphere. "It makes you realize just what you have back there on Earth", said Apollo 8's Jim Lovell. Frank Borman was moved to read from Genesis, Bill Anders took hundreds of photographs of our lush blue-green globe, while Rusty Schweickart marvelled at how the lonesome marble he surveyed through the window of Apollo 9 could contain "all of history and music and poetry and art and death and life and love, tears, joy, games." Later, such longing for home led cosmonauts aboard the Salyut space station to play recordings of Earth sounds – thunder, rain, birdsong – whenever the monotonous hum of their fans got them down.

Over and above the historic first of "getting there", the lasting legacy of the early space program is that it gave us singular insight into the fragility and preciousness of our home planet. It is no accident that the first Earth Day coincided with Apollo's demise; that Anders' photographs became icons of the Earth First! and Whole Earth environmental movements; or that Space Age mystics everywhere began waxing eloquent about the existence of one global soul. Bit by bit, our outbound surge into space was redirected inwards, and from here everything else flowed: Gaia, designer Buddhism, transcendental meditation, the international peace movement, anti-nuclear protests, tree-hugging and rebirthing. The Space Age, in other words, came home to roost on Earth.

At the extreme end of this process sits the "science of Noetics" which not so much internalises as spiritualises space. Noetics is the brainchild of Apollo 14 astronaut Edgar Mitchell, who is perhaps best known for conducting an unauthorized ESP experiment during his mission. Mitchell experienced a kind of cosmic conversion in space, which imbued him with a sense of the interconnectedness of all things and eventually led him to view the all-encompassing void of outer space as a symbol of the unconscious mind. This became the basis of Noetics. The overall message was simple enough: when we gaze out into limitless space, what we are really reckoning with are the vast unmapped territories of the human psyche.

In recent years, Mitchell's conception of extensive, immaterial, shared mental space has found concrete realization in cyberspace – a zero-G environment that is nowhere on Earth. Here, all manner of Space Age-inspired experiments are taking place, from the building of cyber-communities – which, like the space colonies imagined by Gerard O'Neill in the seventies, idealistically offer a sense of belonging to all-comers, regardless of political, racial or religious shadings – to SETI@home, which utilizes distributed networks to process radio signals from space in its continuing search for intelligent life elsewhere.

For the time being, at least, we appear to be more interested in virtual space than in actual space. NASA's 1996 Pathfinder mission to Mars – arguably the biggest hit with the public at large since Apollo – made great play of its virtual credentials, starting before the event with a filmic trailer that portrayed how the bubble-wrapped buggy would bounce across the Martian surface like a piece of hi-tech tumbleweed before coming to rest beside some rocks. The entire mission went on to draw intimately on the model of interactivity well-known to teenage video game addicts everywhere – joy sticks, cartoonish imaging and near-instant command and response functions.

Compared to the thrill of bi-location Pathfinder gave us by allowing us simultaneously to be both on Mars and on Earth, today's space programs seem positively pedestrian. Now that Mir's missions of guile and endurance are at an end, all we're left with is a burgeoning but dull satellite industry, the hit and miss business of launching remote probes and an increasingly unreliable Shuttle, chugging back and forth between the Cape and a still unfinished International Space Station like a dutiful but exhausted work horse. There's not much here to nourish the soul.

Then again, perhaps we need a new mythos for space, one that leaves behind the imagery of colonialism and pioneering, empire-building and alien contact. I don't claim to know what it might look like, but this is where the artistic imagination comes in, inventing new ways of continuing the conversation between outer space and inner space, macrocosm and microcosm, and taking to heart the philosophical insights of space thinkers such as Konstantin Tsyolkovsky and Nicolai Fyoderov, who developed an ideology, cosmism, that envisioned mankind expanding into space, or Carl Sagan, who did so much to turn our thoughts skywards. Not least, there's a fund of intellectual wealth in the quasi-mystical musings of French philosopher Gaston Bachelard, who developed a "poetics of space" on the basis of identifying a correspondence between the immensity of outer space and the inner intensity of human feeling. One thing I do know is that whatever form this new mythos takes, if it is going to hold us in its grip and keep space alive for us, it needs to allow us to continue to reach for the stars.

Being There

Mikhail Ryklin

Hydrolab, Star City
Photo: The Arts Catalyst

At the the beginning of October of 2001, I, along with some European scientists, artists and musicians, had the opportunity to participate in a project in 'Zero Gravity'. Now I belong to a small group of philosophers who have experienced weightlessness. Star City, near Moscow, is an interesting place in itself. A cosmonaut training centre, it also houses a centrifuge, an underwater tank and a planetarium.

The high point of the programme was the parabolic flight. There were ten parabolas on the Ilyushin 76 aircraft, with a total of about five minutes of zero gravity. Cosmonauts also participated in the flight, as it is part of their training programme. All participants had to undertake a medical investigation and safety training in event of emergencies.

Everyone was given a parachute and a flying suit with the Microgravity Interdisciplinary Research logo on it. Most of the participants were carrying out their own projects. My task was perhaps the simplest and at the same time the most elusive. While the other participants had well-planned actions, scientific experiments or were acting out individual "fantasies", my task was simply to reflect on my own state during the different phases of the flight and to correlate the weightless state with the other weight states, without defining weightlessness as anything particularly special. Before the flight we had been warned that you could experience various physical indispositions, so everyone had been nervous and excited.

I barely registered the first two phases of weightlessness. They went by too fast for my consciousness to have time to adapt to this unusual state. But, gradually, from the third parabola, the sensation of weightlessness became more prolonged and more discernable. After a warning signal, bodies began to float into the air. Some participants became euphoric with the experience of discovering new possibilities of making complex jumps, pirouettes, and seeing things fly in air. I experienced a strange feeling, seeing, to my right a professional dancer turning complicated somersaults, to my left two men on flying carpets in orange turbans and red breeches, acting out Eastern fairy tales, and directly beside me another participant throwing up his small daughter's shoes.

I felt like I was experiencing several simultaneous yet incompatible hallucinations. Everything flickered by in separate colour spots, and I tried not to concentrate on one more than the other and to keep a presence of mind. What was equally important was the transition from the state of weightlessness to the state of double gravity. This double load is as interesting as weightlessness. In it, especially at first, you notice your chest and spine experience the doubled weight of your body; the simple raising of a hand in this state represents a substantial physical effort, and my body was literally pressed into the mattresses which covered the floor of aircraft. Both states are interrelated: we enter and leave weightlessness through this double gravity.

I experienced this changed state of consciousness as part of a newly created collective body. I empathised with the participants who became ill (those who vomited). I also tried to count the number of parabolas, but found it difficult. When it seemed to me that there were at least two parabolas still to go, I noticed with that all the other participants in the flight including the cosmonauts and instructors were gathered in the rear of the aircraft for a group photograph. It took me a while to realise that we had already completed the ten parabolas and were returning to the airfield.

Chatting with the members of Flow Motion about our impressions of the flight, I looked at the clock and was surprised to see that over an hour had passed. I had been convinced that everything had not lasted more than 20 minutes, so time had been more than three times compressed! Other participants also said that the flight had been too quick and they had not had time to carry out all the points of their programmes

The changed state of consciousness and the compression of time.

I had nothing planned to make the state of weightlessness something special; when I was weightless, I held onto the horizontal rails which ran along the aircraft's fuselage. Once I took off feet-first to the ceiling where I completed a somersault.

During such a flight, you are acutely aware of your body's relativity: one minute you are flying freely in the air and the next you are lying or sitting down and feeling your increased weight. If you experience enough of these states, you can begin to relate to your usual weight as simply one of the possibilities of your body; it will cease to be the norm. Even a temporary stay in states of weightlessness and double gravity changes one's relation to the body and its terrestrial possibilities.

Between each of the 10 states of suspension and pressure there were three minutes of normal gravity flight. After my consciousness began to function under the constantly changing conditions, it did not return to what I understood as normality during any of the three phases, though during weightlessness a euphoric feeling predominated and it was rather depressive under the double force of gravity.

In this unusual state, spontaneous connections with other people are easily formed. You feel less separated from them, which is probably linked to the compression of time. Hence it is possible to draw the conclusion that we understand our individual selves in the strictly defined conditions of the flow of time. It is worthwhile changing these conditions and making connections with other people who fall beyond the boundaries of our usual perception of the self. And it seems to me that the considerable time dilation (two or more times) also effects one's experience as an individual. The individual is essential and constant by force of habit.

Using weightlessness for pragmatic purposes, for example, in order to extend the motion possibilities of the body and executing movements that which are impossible (for example, several successive somersaults in the air) under normal conditions would have cut off the integrity of my experience, which to me it was important to preserve. This experience helps to develops the intuitive, nonverbal component of our consciousness.

The flight organisers at Star City proved to be likable people, with good English. The flight commander, a Colonel with almost thirty years' experience, had trained many well-known cosmonauts. After the completion of flight the Colonel congratulated us on our entrance into the club of people who had experienced zero gravity.

Star City

In Soviet times, legends circulated about life in Star City: exceptional people lived there, there were special supplies of food and goods, an abundance inaccessible to simple mortals. It is now evident how modest the requirements of Soviet people were and what a revolution in consumption they have been through in the last ten to fifteen years. Star City, by contrast, has remained as it was in the 60s and 70s. Almost everything in it is devoted to the memory of Yuri Gagarin: the training centre for cosmonauts, the Yuri Gagarin cultural centre, the numerous monuments to Gagarin, and the countless photographs of him around the town.

The Russian-Soviet cosmonautics venture had its own romantic, collectivist ideology: the idea that Earth was not the most favourable place for human life; it was a place which it would be desirable to leave when possible. After the launch of the first Sputnik satellite into orbit and the first cosmonaut in space, the Soviet Union partly infected the West with this romantic vision. Space was from now on more than just a field for competition in military technologies, although the West has always been more sceptical about the possibilities of a prolonged stay for humans in space.

In the Soviet Union this romantic notion of the conquest of space was closely linked with the ruling ideology, but it has only been partly replaced by the commercial climate that now prevails in Russia. Flights, like this one are carried out in Star City on average once a month and are considered an exception to the serious work of training professional cosmonauts (which takes about nine years). American astronauts also train in Star City.

A little way from the typically Soviet multi-family apartment blocks, there are two American blocks. There, the cafeteria differs only slightly from the cafeterias of Soviet times: the selection of food is small and it is badly prepared. In the Star City souvenir shop, we saw many Easter eggs with space symbols: additional proof of the idea that Russian cosmism represents a kind of religion; partly completing Russian orthodoxy, partly competing with it.

When Flow Motion gave a performance in the Star City cultural centre – beneath an enormous portrait of Gagarin holding a pigeon of peace against his chest – the audience was mostly children and teenagers from 5 to 18 years. At first, they did not know how react to the combination of techno-music and noise recorded on the aircraft, but then they began in small groups to dance.

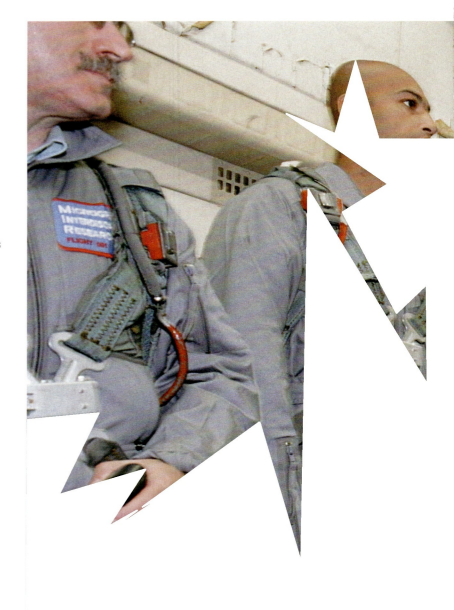

MIR Flight 001. Photo: Alexander Volokhovsky

Against Gravitropism: Art and the Joys of Levitation

Eduardo Kac

Hans Haacke, Sphere in Oblique Air Jet, 1967
Photo: Hans Haacke/ARS New York/VG-Bild-Kunst Bonn

"Gravitropism" means growth in response to gravity.[1] I use the term gravitropism in art beyond its biological origin, to underscore the fact that gravity plays a fundamental role in the forms and events we are able to create on Earth, and that forms and events created in zero gravity to be experienced in the same environment might be radically different. I first wrote about gravitropic forms and events in 1987, while creating and articulating the theory of a new poetic language produced out of light, with protean linguistic events floating and changing in space, freed from material and gravitational constraints. In my original text I stated: "As we experience massless optical volumes -- focused luminous vibrations suspended in the air -- "gravitropism" (form concitioned by gravity) makes way for "antigravitropism" (creation of new forms not conditioned by gravity), freeing the mind from the clichés of the physical world and challenging the imagination".[2] I coined the word "antigravitropism" to retain the affirmative quality of negating or neutralizing gravity.

The powerful gesture of defying gravity in art can be traced back to innovative early twentieth-century sculptors, such as

Calder and Moholy-Nagy. While the first reduced the support of massive structures to a single suspended point with his "Mobiles", the second went as far as experimenting directly with levitation, with absolutely no physical support whatsoever. In his seminal book "Vision in Motion", published posthumously in 1947, Moholy-Nagy appears levitating a chisel with compressed air. The photograph is striking: we see Moholy-Nagy's profile and before him the object suspended in the air with no apparent means of support. In previous books Moholy-Nagy articulated notions about the evolution of sculptural form, suggesting that the virtual volume--volume created optically by the accelerated motion of an object--was a new possibility for sculpture. l

In his film "Design Workshops" (1946), he presented a sequence, less than a minute long, in which coloured ping pong balls float in an air jet. As an artist crossing many discipline boundaries, Moholy-Nagy also considered that in the future the neutralization of gravity could be a useful tool in design. It was not until the 1960s that several of this visionary's ideas would find currency. Hans Haacke's sculpture "Sphere in Oblique Air-Jet" (1967), presents the viewer with precisely what its title indicates: a buoyant balloon that stably hovers in space. The sculpture accomplishes this feat through what is known as Bernoulli's principle, according to which a stream of air (or fluid) has lower pressure than stationary air (or fluid). On a practical level, this means that moving air can create aerodynamic lift.

Although the Hungarian constructivist did not explore this notion in his own sculptures, levitation and the conquest of space attracted the attention of artists working in the 1950s. Lucio Fontana's Spatialist movement, for example, made direct references to space. In 1951 he clearly stated: "Man's real conquest of space is his detachment from the earth". Aaron Siskind's 1950s series of photographs "Terrors and Pleasures of Levitation" present the viewer with contorted and airborne human bodies. These compelling images, which evoke humankind's mythical dream of flying, look as though they could be right out of an astronaut training program. While in both cases it is really the metaphor of space and levitation that is brought to the fore, the use of magnetism to suspend forms in space became the key element in the innovative work of the Greek kinetic artist Takis.

In 1938 Gyorgy Kepes produced a series of photographs and photograms in which he experimented with the visual properties of magnets and iron filings, but it was Takis who, in 1959, introduced the aesthetic of sculptural magnetic levitation with his elegant "Télésculpture". The sculpture is composed of three small conical metal pieces that are attached, through thin wires, to three nails. The three conical pieces are suspended above an irregular plane and levitate in front of a magnet.

Yves Klein, Leap into the Void, near Paris, October 23 1960
Photo: Harry Shunk/ARS New York/ADAGP Paris, DACS London

Aaron Siskind, Terrors and Pleasures of Levitation no. 37, 1953
Collection George Eastman House

Vik Muniz' contribution to En El Cielo, 2001

David Antin, Sky Poems 1987-88

This was the seed of a complex body of work through which this magician of levitation has investigated the expressive power of invisible forces.

In September of 1959, the Moon was first visited by the Soviet spacecraft Lunik 2. As the first probe to impact the Moon, Lunik 2 made evident that human displacement in space was on the horizon. Fascinated by the implications of this idea, Takis realized an event in 1960 at the Iris Clert Gallery, in Paris, entitled "L'Impossible, Un Homme Dans L'Espace" (The Impossible, A Man in Space). Donning a "Space Suit" designed by Takis, wearing a helmet, and attached to a metal rod connected to the floor, Sinclair Belles was "launched" across the gallery onto a safety net. The event orchestrated by Takis pointed to the unknown: the logic and the biologic that govern human existence on Earth will not readily apply to our life in space. Also responding to the visual and intellectual stimulation provided by humankind's first steps beyond the Earth, Yves Klein's "Leap into the Void" (1960) was a photomontage alluding to the new condition of the body considered, rather concretely, in relation to the cosmos (reminiscent as it was of Siskind's series).

It is worth noting that other artists active in the 1960s further elaborated the vocabulary of magnetism. Harvard-educated Venezuelan sculptor Alberto Collie created electromagnetic levitators for innovative sculptures called spatial absolutes. In his sculptures he employed titanium disks that float freely (that is, with no point of attachment) in an electromagnetic field. If the disk budges, a feedback system strengthens the field, thus keeping the disk in its state of equilibrium.

One peculiar approach to the suspension of (ephemeral) forms in space is the use of vaporous substances through a technique known as Skywriting, which consists in the writing or drawing formed in the sky by smoke or another gaseous element released from an airplane, usually at approximately 10,000 feet. In the late 1960s and early seventies, artists such as James Turrell, Sam Francis, and Marinus Boezem started to employ skywriting as a medium. Poet David Antin created skypoems over Los Angeles and San Diego in 1987-1988. These and other artists and writers created evanescent forms within what is known as the troposphere, that is, the lowest atmospheric layer. Pushing the concept of a sky art into the space age, beyond aerial acrobatics and the design of evanescent forms, the

Brazilian artist Paulo Bruscky proposed, in 1974, the creation of an artificial aurora borealis, which according to the artist would be produced by airplanes colouring cloud formations. Bruscky published ads in newspapers to both document the project and inform the public. The ads were also an instrument in his search for sponsors. They were published in the Brazilian papers Diário de Pernambuco, in Recife, September 22, 1974 and Jornal do Brasil, Rio de Janeiro, December 29, 1976. While on a Guggenheim fellowship in New York, he also published ads in the Village Voice, New York, May 25, 1982. The creation of artificial auroras was realized in 1992, not by Bruscky, but by NASA as part of environmental research. Approximately sixty artificial mini-auroras were created by employing electron guns to fire rays at the atmosphere from the space shuttle Atlantis.

The artistic use of skywriting further extended the aerial performances set forth in Futurist manifestos. In addition to the well-known writings of Futurism's founder, Filippo Tommaso Marinetti, of particular relevance is the 1919 manifesto "Futurist Aerial Theatre", by Fedele Azari, in which he wrote: "I HAVE MYSELF PERFORMED, IN 1918, MANY EXPRESSIVE FLIGHTS AND EXAMPLES OF ELEMENTARY AERIAL THEATRE OVER THE CAMP OF BUSTO ARSIZIO. I perceived that it was easy for the spectators to follow all the nuances of the aviator's states of mind, given the absolute identification between the pilot and his airplane, which becomes like an extension of his body: his bones, tendons, muscles, and nerves extend into longerons and metallic wires."

Another significant, albeit little known antecedent, is the "Dimensionist Manifesto", published in 1936 by the Hungarian poet Károly (aka Charles) Sirato and signed by Arp, Delaunay, Duchamp, Kandinsky, Moholy-Nagy, and Picabia, among others. The "Dimensionist Manifesto" was published in Paris as a loose sheet attached to the magazine Revue N + 1. Its most ambitious proposal is four-dimensional sculpture: "Ensuite doit venir la creation d'un art absolument nouveau: l'art cosmique (Vaporisation de la sculpture, theatre Syno-Sens – denominations provisoires). La conquête totale de l'art de l'espace à quatre dimensions (un "Vacuum Artis" jusqu'ici). La matière rigide est abolie et remplacée par des matériaux gazéfiés. L'homme au lieu de regarder les objets d'art, devient lui-même le centre et le sujet de la création, et la création consiste en des effets sensoriels dirigés dans un espace cosmique fermé." This anticipatory vision would become a reality not only through the use of vapours and gases as new art materials

Pierre Huyghe's "L'Expédition Scintillante, Act II: Untitled (light show)", 2002, comes to mind), but through the continuous use of skywriting as a medium in contemporary art, as exemplified by "En el Cielo", an exhibition of skywriting projects created by several artists for the Venice Biennale in 2001 and organized by TRANS, a New York organization that presents experimental art. In spite of its appeal to artists, though, skywriting is itself a vanishing art form, having been largely replaced in the commercial world by a faster sky messaging technique, known as "skytyping", in which several planes fly in formation and use a computer-controlled radio signal to emit puffs of smoke that form letters.

Bruscky's proposal explored a scale greater than the Land Art or the Earthworks typical of the period, since his vision of an artificial aurora borealis would reach millions at once, who would see the work simply by looking up at the sky. By contrast, works that manipulate magnetism or electromagnetism often have a smaller, more intimate scale. If Takis' work has a forceful and raw power that emanates from his unadorned handling of materials such as iron and steel, quite different are the levitation projects by the American artist Thomas Shannon.

Shannon has been creating since the early 1980s a series of sculptures based on materials such as bronze, gold, and marble, as well as painted wood, in which the source of magnetism is not visible. Rather than seeking to make evident the tension that results when opposite poles attract, Shannon's sculptures search for a sense of quiet equilibrium, resting on the visual harmony created by the presence of two basic components: the base and the floating element. Finding in science and natural phenomena a rich source for visual research, Shannon's vocabulary takes levitation into the realm of a reduced articulation of sculptural forms where pairing of objects structures the magnetic experience.

Many developments in twentieth-century art led to a radical reduction in the use of physical matter to form sculptural volume and to support or present this volume in space. From Gabo's constructions (1919/20) to Fontana's perforations, from Moholy-Nagy kinetic works to Calder's mobiles, we have witnessed a movement to liberate modern sculpture from the constraints of enclosed and static form resting on the two-dimensional surface of the pedestal. Artists such as Takis and Shannon -- and the Brazilian sculptor Mario Ramiro, who in 1986 created a self-regulating electromagnetic levitator entitled G0 (standing for "zero gravity") -- have given continuation to this search to release sculpture from gravitropism. In Ramiro's "Gravidade Zero" (Zero Gravity), an electromagnet regulated by a photo-sensor maintains a metallic form floating in space in a state of levitation. Freed from a two-dimensional base, and from any point of support in space, this object is in a truly three-dimensional kinetic space. Ramiro's levitating form presents volume-inversion relations: The area of the object's greater

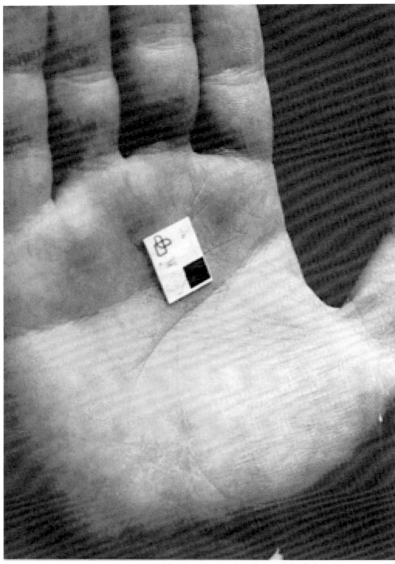

Forrest Myers, Moon Museum 1969, Miniaturised iridium-plated drawing on ceramic wafer
Photo: Forrest Myers

mass can be seen at the top. The lower part, the traditional base of the object, does not need to support the volume above it.

The inevitable conclusion is that zero gravity is the next frontier. Artworks have been taken aboard spacecraft since 1969, when "The Moon Museum", a small ceramic tile with drawings by artists such as Robert Rauschenberg and Andy Warhol, was carried to the Moon aboard a Saturn V rocket on Apollo 12. A significant development was the permanent installation of a sculpture by artist Paul van Hoeydonck (Antwerp, b. 1925) on the surface of the Moon in 1971, also carried on a Saturn V rocket on Apollo 15. Entitled "Fallen Astronaut" (aluminum, 8.5 cm long), the work was placed at the Hadley-Apennine landing site by American astronauts Dave Scott and Jim Irwin (Apollo 15). Next to the sculpture, inserted in the lunar soil is a commemorative plaque, homage to astronauts and cosmonauts who lost their lives in the course of space exploration.

In 1989 Lowry Burgess flew objects on the Shuttle as part of a conceptual artwork entitled "Boundless Cubic Lunar Aperture". These works are significant steps towards an art that engages outer space materially, but they were not created in outer space or conceived specifically to investigate the new possibilities of art in true weightlessness. The first works to do so are the sculpture "S.P.A.C.E.", created outside the Earth by American artist Joseph McShane in 1984 and the sculpture "The Cosmic Dancer", created in 1993 by Arthur Woods, an American artist living in Switzerland.

McShane's work was launched into space on October 5, 1984 aboard the U.S. Space Shuttle Challenger. McShane's piece was produced with the vacuum of space and the conditions of zero gravity and returned to Earth in its altered state. A sphere with a valve and earth atmosphere within was opened once in orbit. The vacuum of space evacuated the sphere, the valve was closed, and the vacuum of space was then contained within. For McShane, the artwork is not the glass object per se, but the containment of outer space within, the potential wonder generated by bringing space vacuum to Earth and to close proximity to viewers.

The question concerning the reception of space art necessarily involves a reflection on the experience of it in space. The primary viewers for "The Cosmic Dancer" lived with the "terrors and pleasures of levitation" in conditions of zero gravity. A sharp-angled form launched to the Mir Space Station on May 22, 1993, "The Cosmic Dancer" stressed the cultural dimension of space since it created the experience of art integrated into a human environment beyond Earth. The video that documents the project shows the two Russian cosmonauts Alexander Polischuk

Arthur Woods, Cosmic Dancer on the Mir Space Station, launched on May 22 1983
Photo: Arthur Woods

and Gennadi Mannakov performing (rotating, hovering, flying) with the sculpture in the confines of Mir, where the sculpture was left. The flaming remnants of the Mir space station plunged into the South Pacific on March 23, 2002.

In the case of Arthur Woods, the performance of the cosmonauts complements his project. As one watches the video documentation, one feels that the cosmonauts stand vicariously for all viewers, that is, all those who in the future will have the opportunity to experience space as a social and cultural milieu, and not only as a research lab. Clearly, the performance of the body in an environment devoid of the forces of gravity is aesthetically rich in its own right.

This very issue has been the focus of French choreographer Kitsou Dubois's work for over a decade. Since 1991 she has been flying in microgravity parabolic flights and exploring the gestural, kinesthetic and proprioceptive potential of weightless dance. She has flown alone as well as with other dancers. Dubois is unique in her relentless investigation of zero gravity. In addition to continuously pursuing new levitation opportunities, she has published extensively on the subject, obtained a Ph.D. with her research as the topic of the dissertation, and recreated her experiences in theatrical as well as installation works. As a by-product of her choreographic work, Dubois has also developed a training method for astronauts based on her new protocols for zero gravity dance.

The spectrum of the live arts in space would be incomplete without theatre. In 1999, the "Biomehanika Noordung" performance was staged by the Noordung Biomechanical Cabinet, directed by Dragan Zhivadinov, high above the Moscow skies onboard a cosmonaut training aircraft. The flight crew consisted of eighteen people: six actors, an audience of eight, the flight director (Peljhan), two cameramen and Zhivadinov himself. A series of ten airborne parabolas, with gravity changes oscillating from normal, to twice the usual, to 30-second microgravity episodes, is not the most conducive temporal structure for a long dramatic play. This posed no problem for director Zhivadinov, whose vision of an abstract theatre is well matched by the experience of weightlessness. Zhivadinov placed a red set on the back of the plane and seats for the audience of eight on each wall of the aircraft. Launched from the stage into the empty space before it, actors wearing brightly coloured costumes performed in a state of levitation, before being pushed down to the floor by gravity changes, and back up in the air again, and so on, as the airplane completed its parabolas. After eight parabolas, Zhivadinov allowed the audience to leave their seats and participate in the euphoric state of bodily suspension, a unique form of audience-actor empathy and, undoubtedly, a new level for the old-age

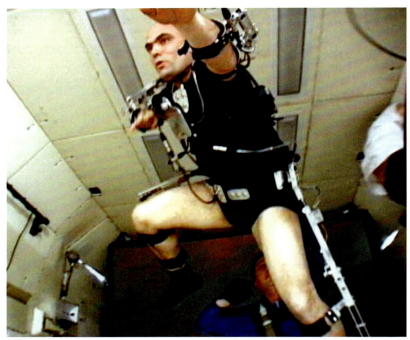

Marcel.lí Antúnez Roca, Dédalus Project 2003
Video still: Panspermia/The Arts Catalyst

dramaturgical device once described by Aristotle as catharsis. While Zhivadinov conceived of the aircraft as a theatrical set, and Woods employed a space station as an ancillary element in the fulfillment of the antigravitropic potential of his sculpture, the media artist, architect, and designer Doug Michaels proposed in 1987 the design of a rather unique space station cum artwork cum "alternative architecture". A co-founder of Ant Farm design group ('68-'78), Michaels was the co-creator of emblematic works of the period, such as Cadillac Ranch (ten cars planted nose down in 1974 in a wheat field located west of Amarillo, Texas) and Media Burn (a 1975 performance in which Michels drove a Cadillac through a pyramid of television sets on fire). In 1986 he established the Doug Michaels Studio to pursue innovative projects in architecture and design. Michaels, who passed away in 2003, developed with his colleagues in 1987 a concept for a spacecraft to host artists and scientists interested in human-dolphins interaction and communication.

The project resonated with the pioneering work of John Lilly, a scientist who defended the idea that dolphins have consciousness and intelligence at a time when this fact was not yet scientifically established. As a result of his research, Lilly went on to author books such as "Man and dolphin" (Garden City, N.Y., Doubleday, 1961), "The Mind Of The Dolphin: A Nonhuman Intelligence" (Garden City, N.Y., Doubleday, 1967) and "Communication Between Man and Dolphin: The Possibilities of Talking With Other Species" (New York: Crown Publishers, 1978). On its January-February issue of 1987, the magazine The Futurist featured Michaels's Project Bluestar, an orbiting "think tank in zero gravity" meant to include both humans and dolphins. According to the proposed design, the marine mammals' ultrasonic emissions would be used to program the central computer.

In 1993, the same year Woods launched "The Cosmic Dancer", the Chinese artist Niu Bo started "The Zero-Gravity Project", which he first pursued in Japan with a plane that flies in parabolic arcs at 20,000-25,000 ft. Bo covered the interior of the plane with rice paper and used a paint produced from the mixture of several elements. To create this paint the artist combined China ink, watercolour, and oil, among other materials, and placed the paint in balloons. During the near weightlessness of microgravity flights, he released the paint. With his "Space Atelier" Bo wishes to convey that just as the Impressionists had to leave their studios to explore the possibilities of natural light, a new culture will be created when artists leave the surface of the Earth.

The Spanish artist and performer Marcel.li Antúnez Roca created Dédalus, a series of microperformances realized in 2003 during two parabolic flights aboard the Ilyushin MDK 76, flown at the Gagarin Cosmonaut Training Center, Star City, Russia. This work was part of a larger project carried out by The Arts Catalyst, Projekt Atol, V2, Leonardo-Olats and other organisations taking part in the MIR (Microgravity Interdisciplinary Research) consortium, which aims to enable artists to work in microgravity conditions. Performing with an exoskeleton wireless interface and the robot Requiem, Roca's involuntary movements activated videos by means of potentiometers in the dresskeleton's circuit. The videos explore themes that the artist considers evocative of an exobiological iconography, such as biochemistry/microbiology, higher transgenic organisms and bio robots.

Artworks such as discussed above open a new realm of speculative inquiry into the future of art in worlds other than the Earth. While we remain confined to the blue planet, three possibilities open up for art that engages what could be called a "zero gravity sensibility".

First, it is clear that the potential for magnetism and electromagnetism in art is far from exhausted. Second, the increasing access to microgravity facilities in Russia will force the opening of new markets in Europe, Japan, and the United States, further enabling more artists and performers to explore weightlessness. Third, as plans for space tourism evolve, actual zero gravity might also become more accessible, albeit at a lower pace, since costs will remain high for the foreseeable future. Space tourism was jumpstarted on April 28, 2001, when the Russian Soyuz-U booster blasted two Russian cosmonauts and a paying tourist, the American millionaire Dennis A. Tito, into orbit for a rendezvous with the International Space Station.

Electromagnetism holds great potential for sculptural levitation. Yet untapped, for example, is a property known as diamagnetism. Diamagnetic materials repel both the north and south poles of a magnet. All materials are weakly diamagnetic, but it is difficult to levitate ordinary objects. However, with a strong magnetic field and strongly diamagnetic materials (such as neodymium magnets and graphite blocks), it is possible to create stable regions for diamagnetic levitation.

Artists seeking to explore levitation beyond magnetism and electromagnetism can investigate advanced techniques presently only found in research laboratories. A high-temperature electrostatic levitator allows the control of heating and levitation independently and, unlike an electromagnetic levitator, does not require that the floating object be a conductor of electric charge. Acoustic levitators enable the suspension of liquids in a state of equilibrium through acoustic radiation force. Also, liquids can be suspended by a gas jet and stabilized by acoustic forces. Superconductor levitators enable objects to float above a magnet in fog of liquid nitrogen. With a laser levitator it is possible to trap gas bubbles in water and create a condition of stable levitation by applying optical radiation pressure of the light beam horizontally and vertically. At last, as levitation touches biology, molecular magnetism is predicated on the application of ordinary but very strong magnetic forces over a regular object. The forces are directed upwards and take advantage of the very weak magnetic response of the object present in the field, enabling the levitation of objects usually not regarded as capable of levitation (such as plastics) and living organisms (plants, insects, small animals – and conceivably humans, if the field could be made strong enough).

The manipulation of the magnetic properties of nanosized objects is also a possibility, which could include macroscopic manifestation of the quantum behavior of these very small objects.

These techniques offer a glimpse into what might be possible when life in the international space station becomes more common, when colonization of the Moon goes from science fiction to science fact, and when the space program overcomes what, in the public opinion, is its most exciting challenge: landing human beings on Mars. The creation of new alloys and compounds in zero gravity and the prospect of interplanetary colonization suggest that space exploration is more than a metaphor in art. It is a material and intellectual challenge that must be met.

1 Gravitropism is a Botany term. Roots have positive gravitropism because they grow in the same direction of gravitational forces (i.e. down). Stems on the other hand have negative gravitropism, as they grow against gravity (i.e. up).

2 Kac, Eduardo. "Sintaxe, Leitura e Espaço na Holopoesia", catalogue of the exhibition "Arte e Palavra" (Word and Image), Forum de Ciência e Cultura, Universidade Federal, Rio de Janeiro, 1987.

Previous versions of this text appeared in: Kostic, Aleksandra (ed.). I Levitate, What's Next... (Maribor, Slovenia: Kibla, 2001), pp. 88-97; and: Space Art, A. Bureaud, J.-L. Soret (dir.), catalogue du Festival @rt Outsiders 2003, numéro spécial, Anomos, Paris, Sept. 2003, pp. 196-199

Rocket pioneer, Wernher Von Braun: 'We can lick gravity, but sometimes the paperwork is overwhelming!'
Photo: Walter Sanders/Time Life Pictures/Getty Images

Achieving Levity

Judith Palmer

In the mid-17th century, a few years after Galileo dropped cannon balls from the leaning tower of Pisa, and a few before Isaac Newton got hit on the head by an apple, an Italian monk called Joseph of Cupertino developed a tendency to levitate while praying, often finding himself floating high above the altar during mass. He subsequently became the patron saint of astronauts, but sadly St Joseph never passed on his gravity-defying secrets – so scientists had to come up with more reliable methods of experimenting with weightlessness.

For the first space scientists of the 20th century, the greatest unknown of space-travel was whether or not the human body could even function without gravity. Would the heart still pump, would the lungs still inflate, would oxygen continue to reach the brain? On 3 November 1957, Laika the Russian spacedog was blasted into orbit onboard Sputnik 2, and barked the news telemetrically back to earth for four days, that mammals could indeed feed and breathe in zero gravity (even if there was as yet no means of bringing them back to terra firma). In 1960, her canine colleagues Belka and Strelka became the first earth citizens to survive a day of weightlessness and return home fit and healthy, showing no ill-effects from their pioneering experience.

Although it had now been shown that humans should be able to survive weightlessness physically, there was still no means of knowing how their mental faculties might be impaired. When Korolev designed the Vostok craft which carried Yuri Gagarin into orbit on 12 April 1961, he arranged for the entire mission to be flown via automatic systems linked to ground control, leaving the cosmonaut not so much as an instrument to read or a switch to flick. It was beyond all expectations when Major Gagarin's voice came crackling through, reporting, 'Weightlessness has begun. It's not at all unpleasant, and I'm feeling fine'.

The reason weightlessness was so feared by the early space programmes, was due to the difficulty of recreating the condition adequately on earth.

Weightlessness is essentially freefall. The moon, our hundreds of man-made satellites, the international space station and the astronauts living upon it, are all in a state of freefall, but instead of falling vertically downwards towards the centre of the earth, drawn by earth's gravitational pull; they are falling on a curved course (or orbit) around the earth.

In the 1950s, Soviet space scientists discovered that they could achieve two to three seconds of weightlessness, by sending objects hurtling down the 28-storey lift-shaft of Moscow State University, inside a specially-designed cage which then slammed into compressed-air buffers at the bottom. Weight is a measure of an object's resistance to gravity, therefore, if an object is falling freely, there is no resistance to gravity, and the object becomes weightless.

Successors to the Moscow University lift-shaft, are modern drop towers such as NASA's microgravity research facility in Cleveland Ohio, where experiments can drop down a 145 metre-deep hole in the ground for five seconds of weightlessness, vacuum-sealed to escape the effects of air friction. (The ZARM tower in Bremen manages nine seconds of weightlessness by first flipping the object upwards using a catapult system.) But the human body is not particularly partial to being dropped down a hole, however much Styrofoam cushioning you pack down the bottom to absorb the impact of its landing. For earth-bound human experimentation in weightlessness, the only option is a parabolic flight – a bucking bronco of an aeroplane ride.

There are four aircraft currently delivering zero gravity parabolic flights. The Russians use a military transporter plane, the Ilyushin-76 MDK (used by the Arts Catalyst for its art-science flights), the European Space Agency have stripped the seats and padded the walls of an Airbus passenger jet; while NASA and commercial outfit the Zero Gravity Corporation fly large converted Boeings. The highly-skilled manoeuvre is the same for all the pilots – flying the plane on a rollercoaster trajectory, up and down, in a series of steep parabolas. Fly 6km up in the air, at 600km per hour, climb suddenly at a 45 degree angle to 9.5km, then take a nose-dive back down again. Weightlessness is achieved at the top-most arc of the parabola, not just as the plane falls, but also at the top of the climb, as a kind of prolonged hump-back bridge moment.

A parabolic flight offers tantalisingly short periods of weightlessness, only 25-30 seconds at a time – but for those moments, anything untethered within the cabin goes into freefall, floating in mid-air. (Usually, a trace of gravity remains, making it technically not 0g but microgravity.) On either side of that moment of reduced gravity, at each point of acceleration, there is also a period where gravity is almost doubled, and the body becomes heavier, weighed down by the pressure of 1.8g. By flying slightly modified arcs, the pilot can also create a range of different gravitational conditions, allowing passengers to pass through moon gravity (a sixth of earth's gravity) and martian gravity (one third of the gravity experienced on earth).

I once asked the Russian cosmonaut Sergei Krikalev what space smells like. You can detect the scent of it on the outside of your space suit, apparently, after you've come in from a session of extra-vehicular activity. Krikalev admitted that he'd spent many

St Joseph of Cupertino, patron saint of astronauts

hours on board Mir mulling this over, and had eventually succeeded in identifying it, deciding: "space smells like two stones being struck together."

But actually, things don't necessarily smell the same in space as they do down on earth. When a miniature rose bush was grown in microgravity onboard the shuttle Discovery, and the fragrance it had produced was sampled, it was found to have produced a different scent from the control sample grown simultaneously on the ground. Freed from gravity, the chemical composition of the flower's volatile oils had critically altered. (The new aroma molecules, known as 'space rose' note, were synthesised on earth, and eventually made their debut in a perfume called Zen by Shiseido.)

Gravity obscures the underlying behaviour and structure of many chemical compounds and natural phenomena. By removing the gravity, scientists have unmasked the complex structures of HIV proteins and insulin crystals, cracked some of the perplexing propensities of ice floes, sand dunes and cloud formations. Away from an earthbound flat-bottomed petri-dish, new 3-dimensional cell-clusters can be cultured, growing collagen for corneal grafts or culturing heart muscle cells to patch up a damaged heart.

The space pioneers were right to be wary of weightlessness. The absence of gravity subtly alters almost every earthly thing. Leukaemia cells don't seem to reproduce in space, yet bacteria can grow up to 10 times faster than on earth. In weightlessness, astronauts' hearts shrink, muscles atrophy and bones weaken, because the space traveller's body has nothing to push against – and yet these body modifications are only of consequence once the astronaut returns to earth – in zero gravity this is a healthy state of 'space normal'.

Journalist Emma Jane Kirby in flight
Video still: The Arts Catalyst

On the Use and Abuse of Microgravity for Life

Kodwo Eshun

'Our bodies comprise a centre of mass that goes so far beyond the span of our footprints that falling is an unavoidable outcome of pedestrian navigation. Just by standing, we travel around earth's axis at an average of just below 1000 miles per hour, spinning around the sun at close to 66,000 miles per hour, (19 miles per second) and moving farther around the center of our galaxy at close to 660, 000 miles per hour. But our feet are not holding us up as much as the duel between the centripetal forces pulling us toward earth and the centrifugal ones working to throw us off.'
Joseph Lanza, Gravity: Tilted Perspectives on rocketships, rollercoasters, earthquakes and angel food.

'By changing space, by leaving the space of' one's usual sensibilities, one enters into communication with a space that is psychically innovating. For we do not change place, we change our nature.'
Gaston Bachelard, The Poetics of Space

'The foundations of our lives do not themselves have foundations'.
Wittgenstein, Philosophical Investigations.

Given the fact that gravity locates the human species in a condition of subjective verticality, the variable forces of weightlessness and increased g-load imply a fundamental rethinking of the conditions of ground and foundation. From Descartes to Nietzsche, Heidegger to Wittgenstein and Sartre to Derrida, philosophers have analysed modernity in terms of the loss of being, ground, orientation, balance and stability. Groundlessness and its related conditions of rootlessness, homelessness and void epitomise a post-religious universe in which foundational monotheism has collapsed. Microgravity therefore is not so much a metaphor of the human condition in the modern era as a literalisation of the metaphors that inform the history of theology, politics, poetics and philosophy. As an intensively dynamic space-time event, microgravity actualizes concepts central to Western philosophy, concepts that precede and inform the terms of (in)habitable space. To be more precise, microgravity cannot help but materialise dimensions of the metaphysical, the ontological, the theological and the political. When gravity becomes a variable, metaphysics comes down to earth and into the mouth.

For these reasons, the non-place of microgravity is never far from questions of fundamental import. Far from being a zone restricted to a narrowly defined sector of 'sci-art', the experience of a constant such as gravity becoming a variable can be understood in several ways, not only in philosophical terms but also as the realization of the post-war tradition of defamiliarisation.

Microgravity can be seen as a counter-environment in McLuhan's sense, that is to say, as a space that allows us to detach from, and thereby gain insight into a fundamental force that surrounds us, a force we remain as unaware of as a clownfish of water in its aquarium. The parabolic flight that enables variable gravity inside the aeroplane cabin might be seen as constituting a variation upon that which theorist Hakim Bey calls a zone of temporary autonomy; equally it might be understood as a space-time capable of creating a distinctive kind of alienation effect, to use Brecht's term. The kind of alienation from the habitual that is familiar in variable gravity might in turn induce vivid kinds of disalienation back on land, where one begins to re-experience gravity, and therefore normality as if for the first time. The surprise of leaving your pen in microgravity where it remains, poised, in mid-air, is matched only by the curious sight of watching it drop from air to surface. For a while then, the agravic time-space can become a point of singularity from which one sets off on a journey to what Holger Czukay calls 'the peak of normal'.

Perceiving gravity as the peculiarity it is implies an insight into the ways in which such a habitual force actively participates to form our consciousness. Variable gravity thereby allows us to dramatise ontological, ideological, poetic and political questions from a number of traditions. The experience of an absolute becoming a variable does not only point to traditions of destabilization; it also implies the kinds of histories that organize themselves around the 'need to reconstruct certain kinds of stability' in Toni Morrison's words.

These might be characterized as reconstruction programs for living that emerge from the context of instability, disorientation and imbalance endemic to the post-colonial aftermath of refugees, migrants and diasporic citizenship. It is not simply that everyone becomes an alien in variable gravity; rather that the actualities of such an alien time-space suspend normality in such a way as to provide revelation through a continual logic of reversal. Microgravity is an event whose singularity destroys all metaphor and in so doing allows a thousand allegories to bloom.

At this point in time, nothing could be easier than to sketch out a trajectory of 20th Century cultural activity informed by gravitropic impulses to leave behind this Earth. Fuelled by longings for aspiration, elevation and utopia, such a tendency would be informed by the sensibility that cultural phenomenologist Gaston Bachelard (in Air and Dreams: An Essay on the Imagination of Matter) terms the 'ascensional psyche' . We could discern this gravitropic will in the work of cyberneticists such as Manfred Clyne, artists such as Malevich, Haacke, Levine and Matta-Clark, sculptors such as Takis, architects such as Leonidov, Krutikov and Buckminster Fuller, novelists such as Samuel R.Delany and Colson Whitehead and composers such as Sun Ra. Such an inventory would only hint at future lines of investigation into what we might call 'the gravic imaginary.' This inventory might in turn allow us to place overlapping genealogies in a series of productively inconclusive dialogues: Afrofuturology might encounter Russian Cosmicism, Kinetic Art could be rethought in relation to the New Wave of Science Fiction while Constructivist Architecture might be unframed through Cosmic Jazz.

What is more compelling however is to begin to explore how cultural activity proceeds when faced with the actualities of microgravity that not only fail to fulfill inherited philosophical traditions and artistic expectations but exceed, deviate and swerve from inexact analogies with the everyday. Faced with experiences that partially exceed earthbound life, one would expect the norms of language that support epistemological certainties to partially unravel. The question would then become the degree to which such an unframing could escape reorientation via space medicine that acts as a guarantee of the knowable limits of agravic space. Introducing artistic projects, however defined, into an agravic container, becomes interesting to the extent that distinct kinds of authorities becomes entangled with other kinds of knowledges, thereby creating the potential for unknowing. Such unravellings would seem peculiarly suited to a contemporary artworld preoccupied with trajectories of the nomadic, the interdisciplinary and the temporary.

In the last decade, encounters with the agravic have tended to occur under the sign of science/art. Whatever the successes and failures of science/art and its offspring of space art, it is clear that the insights and the risks of the ongoing dialogic encounter of art and science are magnified within the encapsulated space of variable gravity. There is nowhere to hide in Zero G; as a field of force, it often feels more compelling in and of itself than anything any artist can bring to it.

Over the last decade, cultural agencies (principally the Arts Catalyst) have infiltrated the field of microgravity research once restricted to military astronautics, cosmonautics and space medicine. Artists from fields such as choreography, sculpture, conceptual art, sound art, cybercultural performance and the moving image have been privileged and fortunate enough to participate in parabolic flights. What interests us here however is not so much specific projects but rather the wider conceptions of and attitudes towards this time- space that shape recent interdisciplinary practice.

Given the powerful philosophical, artistic and utopian currents that animate these encounters, it might be useful to initiate a critical inventory of what to date has been a peculiarly under-theorised sector of contemporary art practice. Such an outline therefore does not attempt to survey the entire scene by any means; instead, it seeks to point to the distinctive kinds of conceptualisation that emerge from an encounter that is inimical, if not hostile to the inherited vocabularies of time and space. An outline such as this thereby seeks not to confirm what is already known but to point to and to encourage the different kinds of unknowing, unframing and unbelonging. From such a perspective, microgravity interdisciplinary research, which, despite itself, can often appear hermetic, may be seen to exist at the nexus of contemporary artistic practice. Its concern with intensities, with ephemerality, with affects, with unknowing, with technical transfer, with displacement and unbelonging, are all central concerns of 21st Century culture. Perhaps, here, under acknowledged and barely noticed, peculiar perspectives on the present are emerging.

Speaking from an intense investment in this field, I can affirm that the encounter with altered gravity is an overwhelming and thrilling one that obliges one to learn what the novelist Georges Perec called a new 'species of space'. Given the sensorial experiences of bodily incoherence and proprioceptive confusion, of losing nearly but not quite all sense of body weight, of temporal and pupil dilation, of blood rising and skin tingling, of feeling superheroic, newly born, close to nausea and euphoria, perhaps it is not so surprising that artists often choose to approach such an altered field of time-space as a playground in which to delightedly examine one's experiences. In its initial state, variable gravity is inevitably experienced as a zone of regressive infantilism. The question then becomes how and what one does with this quantity of energy. One can see two distinct responses to this query, each of which presumes a particular stance towards the condition of matter, the nature of the event and the form of the document.

One kind of practice seeks to tap into the unstable media of the agravic field. The corporeal excitability of imbalance, of entangled legs, shoulders, arms, torsos and hair is channelled into a synchronized series of bodies whose serene severity calms and clarifies the watchful eye of the non-participant. Training in the sense of normative balance that space medicine calls 'the subjective vertical' allows the artist to tap into the temporary dynamics of turbulence that animate time-space.

What is compelling here is the spatial attitude implied, namely a certain humility towards a distinctive space-time that is not so much post-human as para-human in its predictable unpredictablity. The aim is to encourage a reorientation of consciousness through a kind of arte povera translated into agravic time-space. Practices that are chastened, minimal, simplified, weakened or barely there at all are undertaken so as to allow variable gravity to make the human body its subject, to make the earthbound life its object, to actively participate in the production of consciousness. The idea is to place expertise at the service of gravity so that modes of behaviour and consciousness which are determinate yet unknowable in advance may begin to emerge.

Another kind of work seeks to impose a spectacle upon this partially alien zone. Such an approach tends to favour elaborate high-tech hardware. As a result it finds itself unable to respond to variations in force and therefore functions much as it would on earth. The attitude here is to master the paraspace of microgravity in order to confirm the authority of the body in an unfamiliar context.

It is clear that the first approach offers more scope and play than the second; yet the former aesthetic of transplanted arte povera and the latter aesthetic of theatrical spectacle are linked by a mutual indifference to the multiple spatial, environmental, military, architectural, geopolitical and historical contexts within which parabolic flights take place.

One way of characterising the attitudes of the first five years of art in parabolic flight is to see practices as the exploration of an individualised conception of matter. This self-absorption necessarily implies decontextualisation and ahistoricism.

What is intriguing today is the beginnings of a reaction against this, a countervailing response visible in the practice of certain artists. It is likely that the next five years of interdisciplinary practice will see more artists turn towards the question of historicity. The degree of unknowing generated within the aeroplane is complicated when it is connected to the multiple frames and narratives that bear down upon and extend the singularity of the event. The days of the artist playing the innocent in zero gravity are gone forever, never to return. The result of the turn towards different kinds of agravic histories will instead be experimental projects that link experience to context, interior to exteriority, event to memory, intensity to historicity, encounter to futurity, the microcosm of microgravity to the macrocosm of geopolitical crisis in ways yet to be discovered.

The most immediate connection between the inside and the outside of the aeroplane, between the encounter and futurity is the document, the moving image that is filmed onsite and screened offsite. Indeed, the audience's primary interface with art in parabolic flight is through and with the digital video as document. Perhaps this explains why many artists tend to present video documents of their agravic encounter as if they were scientists presenting evidence and the artwork merely a delivery system for demonstrating a scientific procedure. Such a positivist conception of the moving image underwrites the attitude to matter and to the event familiar in both kinds of practice I have outlined.

In reaction to this, we can foresee a time when the process of digital filming and the moving image as digital document become experimental practices which test the hypothesis that variable gravity offers a degree of immersion within the disorientation of the geopolitical. To turn away from monofocal visions of gravity towards complex narratives that embed agravic time-space within multiple notions of time, space and event necessitates a much more sophisticated approach towards the moving image. The emphasis on the evidentiary image will give way to notions of the image influenced by the kinds of reconfiguration of the document and of the archive that can be seen across the contemporary artistic landscape

Such a reconfiguration can be seen in the return to and extension of the forms of the video-essay and the essay-film. Both the video-essay and the essay-film seek to complicate the document by considering questions of the indexical present, the nature of the event, the behaviour of matter and the role of memory. By opening microgravity interdisciplinary research to the notion of fabulation that exists within and between the domains of fact, fiction and documentary, perhaps a new gravic imaginary may emerge that would be distinct from and yet related to the postwar lineage we indicated earlier on. This, at least is clear: the escapism of the first heroic explorations into the force field of the agravic now looks antiquated. What is needed is practices that suspend the instinct to escape, stretch that moment, and in so doing, allow singular affects to emerge. In this hiatus between unknowing and consciousness, perhaps modes of being may emerge that navigate temporality in unforeseen ways. In so doing, future artists may begin to reconstruct certain fragile kinds of stability.

Images: Biomehanika Noordung

Projekt Atol Flight Operations –

Overview of the backend of seven micro and variable gravity experimental flights from 1999-2003 and the start of the ARTYOM-MM satellite development

Marko Peljhan

Projekt Atol Flight Operations (PA-FO) is a branch of Zavod Projekt Atol, an independent arts and research organization founded in 1994 and based in Ljubljana, Slovenia. PA-FO was founded in June 1999 to organize and support the parabolic flights of the Cosmokinetical Kabinet Noordung performances, *Biomehanika Noordung,* in conjunction with the Gagarin Cosmonaut Training Centre (GCTC) in Star City.

First 3 Flights – Training and Biomehanika Noordung

PA-FO organized a training flight in August 1999 and two performance flights, with eight members of the public, in December 1999. The two December flights took place successively, after refuelling and change of the audience members of the crew, 1 actor and 1 cameraman. PA-FO oversaw the development of the flight architecture design, the preflight planning and coordination, safety procedures, technological systems setup, the intercom systems development, overall production and logistical plans, as well as managing the crew and guest-crew on board the experimental aircraft. Flight grade equipment had to be installed and tested, together with specially designed seats for the audience, capable of sustaining accelerations of up to 10g over a period of 20 seconds (ten times the force of gravity). The design of the seats and set was done by the Noordung design team, with Stasa and Dunja Zupancic, together with Andraz Torkar, while the safety modifications were done under the review of Cpt. Stepanov of the GCTC and his flight laboratory crew.

The flights were organized within the GCTC structure and under the responsibility of the cosmonaut training department, headed by Col. Grekov and Col. Ren, with Cpt. Stepanov as the main liaison and Col. Irina Sokolova as interpreter and crew-training officer.

The *Biomehanika Noordung* performances (directed by Dragan Zhivadinov), which took place during both the August and December flights, were based on the dramaturgical plot, following a science text on bone structure transformation that takes place in microgravity and had 10 parabolas both in dramaturgical and physical senses. The whole work was also part of the larger and more complex aesthetic mythology created by the director and his team within the context of his Cosmokinetical Kabinet Noordung group. The training flight in August was designated as the "farewell ritual" for Marko Mlacnik, an actor taking part in the "50-year project" – a project of 6 performance repetitions (1995, 2005, 2015, 2025, 2035, 2045) and the launching of 16 small GEO satellites that will serve as "substitute actors" until 2045. (Farewell rituals are short dramatic forms that are to take place between the repetitions of the 50-year performance cycle, and in the case that some of the actors taking part in the performance pass away as the performance evolves, they will be replaced by robotic satellites – "substitute actors" in space and robotic avatars in the performance on earth. In 2045 all the actors are presumed dead, and the performance will continue in its satellite form in space.)

Seven actors in total participated in the performance, which was viewed by 16 members of the audience, thus making Biomehanika Noordung the first microgravity theatre performance complete with audience in history.

During the two flights in December of 1999, a scientific experimental payload was also carried on board, consisting of 12 containers with different malign cancer-cell cultures with the focus on specific protein kinases identification and possible functional change observation. The experiment was the result of an open call to scientists in Slovenia to design flight – grade projects to be flown for free on the already financed art – based flights. The flight and post-flight cell culture extraction and freezing were carried out by myself in conjunction with the Oncological Institute of the Ljubljana Clinical Centre.

These first flights, together with the PA-FO work on satellite development, that started in 1998 as part of an effort within the then still cryptic "World-Information.Org" organisation in Vienna with the Public Netbase (the initiative involved research into the Surrey University of Technology and Berlin Technical University satellite development and command and control programs), and our collaboration with the TsUP in Korolev during the Kristal MIR mission in May 1998 served as the initial push for the foundation of the Slovene Space Agency by myself, Primoz Pislak and Zhivadinov. The goal being to set up an independent space research agency in Slovenia, which would combine the work of artists and scientists in aerospace and related fields on equal terms and thus provide a unique opportunity and perspective on the form that a small modern country space agency could have. This would be the first institution of its kind in our country and for its unique interdisciplinary mission, in the world.

The initiative was presented to the wider public in the spring of 2001, during the Noordung Forum event at the Slovenian Academy of Arts and Sciences and work on its institutional framework is proceeding with the identification of existing research in Slovene institutes with potential space and space related applicability in science, engineering and the arts.

Biomehanika Noordung, 1999

Arts Catalyst / MIR Consortium Flights

We invited Rob La Frenais of Arts Catalyst to take part in the first training flight in 1999, the reason being that Arts Catalyst was already involved in the pioneering work of zero gravity choreographer Kitsou Dubois at the time and that new opportunities had opened up with the possible utilisation of Russian hardware and operations for art centred work. This visit and the flight (discussed in detail also in this volume) prompted further discussions regarding possible future collaborations on microgravity/variable gravity parabolic flights between PA-FO, GCTC and Arts Catalyst, resulting in 4 more flights in the following 3 years.

The first PA-FO / Arts Catalyst organised flight took place in September 2000 for the performance company of the choreographer Kitsou Dubois, with a number of other invited artists and scientists participating. This successful collaboration prompted the two organisations to consider a long-term project to enable other artists to access this research space and to visit Star City.

The idea for the establishment of the MIR network was thus born. The network's name (which stands for Microgravity Interdisciplinary Research) clearly defines the goals, while the acronym makes reference to the Russian Space program and the late Mir space station, which was, in its last years, a truly international program. The Mir station was finally de-orbited on March 23, 2001, and in September of that year the pilot MIR flight organised by Arts Catalyst and PA-FO took place, consisting of a mixed British and Russian crew. A presentation of the initial PA-FO flights already took place in the V2 in the spring of 2001, with MIR being born soon afterwards as a collaborative effort between Arts Catalyst, V2, Leonardo-OLATS, Projekt Atol, and the Multimedia Complex of Actual Arts, Moscow. Two MIR flight campaigns have been organized up to now, the MIR Flight 001 in 2001 and MIR Campaign 2003, consisting of two more flights and the work presented in this volume is a tentative reflection on that period and body of work.

ARTYOM-MM

PA-FO is also continuing its work of coordinating the design and launch of the Artjom-MM LEO satellite, designed by Dunja Zupancic and Laurent Paul Robert, with a communications and remote-sensing payload designed by Pact Systems. The project is conceptually part of the activities planned by the Cosmokinetical Kabinet Noordung group, with this first LEO satellite introducing the concept for further developments until 2045 (when the project is planned to end). This satellite will also be the first Slovenian Space Agency satellite project and is planned to serve as a communications and remote-sensing asset of the world tactical media community. The launch is planned in conjunction with the Makeyev design bureau and possibly the AMSAT organization. Talks on defining the satellite began in 2002, with a tentative launch date set for 2012.

All this said, independent or independent-based access to space and space assets, as well as their cultural, creative and tactical media use, is seen as a crucial development and promise, both in technical and political terms for the next decade of space operations, since the transnational nature of the space and orbital expanses has to be used to the benefit of humankind in its totality. Projekt Atol Flight Operations plans to join forces with all institutions and individuals interested in furthering these goals and to actively work on accessing and understanding space-related technologies and paradigms, through the activities of MIR as well as through collaboration with space agencies and space-related technology and policy organizations.

Glossary:

PA-FO: Projekt Atol Flight Operations

GCTC: Yuri Gagarin Cosmonaut Training Center, Star City, Russia

NOORDUNG: Space flight pioneer of Slovenian descent, author of the book "The Problem of Space Travel: The Rocket Motor", 1929

TsUP: (Tsentr Upravlyenyi Polyotov) Center for Flight Control in Korolev, Russia

ARTYOM-MM: First LEO satellite of the planned 16 satellite constellation

LEO: Low Earth Orbit.

patch, Slovenian Space Agency

A Partial History of Parabolic Flight
(and of feeling sick)

Louise K. Wilson

Anthony Bull, Major Boris Naidyonov
Photo: Alexander Volokhovsky

1571

Birth of German astronomer Joannes Kepler who first calculated the exact laws of motion of the planets, their orbits and ellipses and after whom the 'Keplerian trajectory' (aircraft flight path which describes a parabola) is named.

1638

The publication of the story **The Man in the Moone** by Bishop Francis Godwin in which strange birds called Gansas migrated to the moon. Some argue the story contains the first description of the idea of weightlessness in space

"I found then by this Experience that which no Philosopher ever dreamed of, to wit, that those things which wee call heavie, do not sinke toward the Center of the Earth, as their naturall place, but as drawen by a secret property of the Globe of the Earth..."

1865

In his novel **From the Earth to the Moon**, Jules Verne predicted that three men travelling in a bullet-shaped projectile to the moon would experience a weightless state.

"...that day, about eleven o'clock in the morning, Nicholl having accidentally let a glass slip from his hand, the glass, instead of falling, remained suspended in the air.
"Ah!" exclaimed Michel Ardan, "that is rather an amusing piece of natural philosophy."

1883

In the manuscript **Free Space** (first published in 1956) visionary and pioneer of cosmonautics Konstantin E. Tsiolkovsky described ways of motion in zero gravity. He made a drawing of a spacecraft for Free Space depicting cosmonauts in weightlessness

"The Earth is the cradle of the mind, but we cannot live forever in a cradle" Konstantin E. Tsiolkovsky, 1911. (From a letter)

1939

German scientist Heinz von Diringshofen was an important pioneer in air medicine and had constructed a centrifuge to study the effects of centrifugal forces on physiology. He was an enthusiastic pilot and took his test subjects flying, rewarding them with 7 – 8 seconds of weightlessness. He stopped his experiments in this year and devoted himself to training air medicine specialists.

1940

During this year, the effect of weightlessness during flight manoeuvres was 'discovered' by Dr. Heinz von Diringshofen of Berlin, Germany, with high performance aircraft

1946

Parabolic flights began in France. At that time, the French flight test centre (the CEV) used them to test aircraft equipment.

1948

The first test subject for zero gravity experimentation was a monkey at the White Sands Testing area. It was launched in an adapted V2 rocket on a free fall trajectory. The monkey survived the flight unharmed but died on impact when the parachutes failed to open.

By the end of the 1940s, the Russians were working on a civilian research programme into the effects of weightlessness on living creatures.

1950

In a scientific article, Drs. Fritz and Heinz Haber, two scientists employed at the School of Aerospace Mecicine (US) described the possibility of reduced G-force and zero-G force parabolic flights.

1951

At Edwards Air Force Base (AFB), California several Air Force test pilots, including Scott Crossfield and Chuck Yeager, flew parabolic trajectories and experienced weightlessness for up to 20 seconds, even though restrained in their seats.

During zero-G Crossfield reported initial "befuddlement" but with no serious loss of muscle co-ordination while Yeager described a sensation of falling and feeling "lost in space". Physicians and psychologists called this latter response "disorientation"

1952

Experiments began on the effects of reduced-G flights on various animals, such as mice and chimpanzees. These experiments took place at various US Air Force bases, such as Brooks (San Antonio, Texas), Wright-Paterson (Ohio), and Holloman (New Mexico).

In May a test was made using an American Aerobee rocket containing 2 mice and 2 monkeys. There was complete weightlessness inside the capsule for three minutes. The programme ended that year and the US concentrated on developing ballistic missiles for the next 6 years

Argentina conducted parabolic flights from 1952-4 using South American water turtles as test subjects.

1955

A permanent reduced-G/zero-G testing program for humans was inaugurated in August at Holloman Air Force Base (AFB). Eventually the human subjects were subjected to free-floating weightlessness in a specially designed cargo aircraft, such as the KC-135.

1957

Soviet dog **Laika** became the first living creature fired into space on November 3 on **Sputnik 2**, a craft no bigger than a washing machine. In 2002 at the World Space Congress in Houston it was announced that **Laika** had died of fright just after take-off. Previously Russian authorities had circulated reports that the dog survived in orbit for four days.

1959

By now almost 100 people had participated in the experiments at Holloman AFB. Some subjects become quite ill; others, especially experienced test pilots, showed no adverse effects from prolonged weightlessness.

1961

On January 31 a chimpanzee called **Han** became the first American space passenger inside a Mercury capsule. The flight ended after 16 minutes

On April 12 Major Yuri Gagarin became the first man in space aboard **Vostok I**. Gagarin had first experienced weightlessness as a trainee cosmonaut in the back seat of a MiG-15 fighter aircraft flying parabolas.

US Astronaut Alan Shephard made a fifteen minute suborbital flight in **Freedom 7** on May 5. He reported no feelings of discomfort during the five minutes of weightlessness.

1962

On February 20 John Glenn flew the first US orbital flight. One of the goals of the flight was to investigate human sensory reactions to weightlessness.

Some experts predicted that after a few hours in zero-g Glenn's eyes would gradually lose their shape and he would in effect go blind, others predicted that the fluid in the internal ear would start behaving unpredictably. Glenn was however unperturbed.

1963

On June 16 Valentina Tereshkova (code name "Sea Gull") became the first woman and sixth cosmonaut to orbit the Earth. She found weightlessness "not unpleasant"

MIR Campaign 2003
Photo: Panspermia

1965

On March 18 Cosmonaut Alexei Leonov performed the first space walk lasting twelve minutes and nine seconds.

Ed White became the first American to walk in space three months later. Between 1960 and 1962, he estimated he must have flown around 1200 parabolas logging about 5 hours weightlessness when piloting many parabolic flights.

The Mattel Company released Astronaut Barbie, a 10-inch plastic doll dressed in a silver space suit

1968

American astronauts first reported motion sickness during the **Apollo 8** moon voyage. Mission commander Frank Borman became ill on the journey out and refused to undergo tests for motion sensitivity back on Earth. NASA said only that he had suffered a reaction to sleeping pills.

1969

On July 21 American astronauts landed on the moon. Pilot of the Command Module on **Apollo 11** Michael Collins wrote in his autobiography **Carrying the Fire** about his zero-g experiences in a KC-135,
"Flying in space turned out to be easier than flying in the zero-g airplane. It was also a lot more pleasant…There is something very unsettling, even for experienced aviators, about repeating forty or fifty parabolas, the body alternating constantly between zero and 2Gs. Some astronauts threw up. I never quite did, but I was close enough at times to be utterly miserable."

1971

The record of 125 parabolas performed in one flight was set by the US Air Force.

1973

The US space station Skylab was launched to serve as an experiment in long-duration human spaceflight. During the Skylab 3 mission, an astronaut crew spent two months in orbit conducting a busy schedule of experiments, after an initial occurrence of motion sickness. Studies included a student experiment that demonstrated that spiders could spin webs in weightlessness.

1995

Premier of Ron Howard's film **Apollo 13** (Imagine Films) which includes sequences filmed in weightlessness. The film team did some 500 takes aboard the 'Vomit Comet' over four-plus weeks of flying. On one occasion a camera operator threw up on actor Bill Paxton.

1999

Release of the porn film trilogy **The Uranus Experiment** (Private Media Group), directed by John Millerman. Part One is reputed to contain the first explicit sex scene shot in zero gravity conditions. The performers Sylvia Saint and Nick Lang, who portray astronauts, were only allowed one 20-second moment of zero-g to complete the scene. The filming process was described as "particularly messy from a technical and logistical standpoint"

2000

Robert Lepage's solo theatre piece **The Far Side of the Moon** explores sibling rivalry, self-discovery, technology and outer space. The production includes a sequence of simulated weightlessness when Lepage slowly rolls on the floor beneath a large angled mirror in which the viewer sees his 'floating' reflection

2001

With a flight on Soyuz to the International Space Station, the American businessman Dennis Tito becomes the first space tourist. Tito became sick due to weightlessness about four hours after lift-off, "unfortunately, hygienic bags were not properly packed in Soyuz, so we had to use hygienic napkins," said Mission Commander Talgat Musabayev.

Bibliography

Life at the Extremes: the science of survival
by Frances Ashcroft
(Flamingo, 2001)

Carrying the Fire: An Astronaut's Journeys
by Michael Collins and Charles Lindbergh
(Cooper Square Press 2001)

Starman: the Truth behind the Legend of Yuri Gagarin
by Jamie Doran and Piers Bizony
(Bloomsbury London 1999)

On the Shoulders of Titans: A History of Project Gemini
by Barton C. Hacker and James M. Grimwood
(NASA 1977)

Almost Heaven: the story of women in space
by Bettyann Holtzmann Kevles
(Basic Books, 2003)

This New Ocean: A History of Project Mercury
by Loyd S. Swenson Jr., James M. Grimwood and Charles C. Alexander
(Published as NASA Special Publication-4201 in the NASA History Series, 1989)

The Right Stuff
by Tom Wolfe
(Picador 1991)

U.S. Human Spaceflight; A Record of Achievement, 1961–1998
by Judy Rumerman.
NASA Monograph in Aerospace History No. 9 July 1998.

Weightless video
(ESA production, 1998)

www.technovelgy.com

www.cnes.fr/html/_455_461_1365_1366_.php

Ilyushin-76 MDK
Photo: The Arts Catalyst

Projects

MIR Flight 001
Photo: Nicola Triscott

Kitsou Dubois

Gravity Zero, performance, 1994
Kitsou Dubois: A Dancer in Weightlessness, film, 1995
Gravity Zero, video installation, 1999
Fluid Trajectory, video, 2001
Fluid Trajectory, video installation, 2001
Fluid Trajectory, performance, 2002
File/Air, video installation, 2003
The Dancer, the Chair and her Shadow, performance, 2003
Analogies, performance, 2004

For several years, Kitsou Dubois has been developing a process of experimental movement performed in an environment of altered gravity conditions.

As a choreographer and movement researcher, Dubois has carried out the most meticulous, as well as the most immediately appealing, artistic work yet undertaken in the new space of microgravity. In her films and installations, she demonstrates a mastery over the volatile medium of weightlessness. With focused pre-flight training techniques and disciplined dancers, her choreography tames the adrenalin-fed wayward tendencies of bodies in weightlessness and forms them into shapes of apparently effortless beauty

In her extensive research in over 13 years, Kitsou Dubois has identified key references in zero gravity movement, such as the subjective vertical, continuous motion, the consciousness of a "space between", and has explored these on earth, in water and on a trampoline. Central to her work are the video images of parabolic flight experiments that serve as a "memory trace" for the body's movement, enabling the dancers to reassemble a continuity of memory of the dance in weightlessness. Her performances, which are in themselves explorations of these movement references, integrate work in water, floor and trampoline with films from parabolic flight.

In the new space of weightlessness, there is no need for a sense of balance. Indeed, the balance mechanisms of the body are "switched off", and sensations of bodily weight also disappear. Extremities of the body feel less defined and there is a sense of merging with the empty space around. The unstable unknown becomes the reference point (some cope with this better than others). In Kitsou Dubois' choreographic and visual process, the weightless body becomes the symbol for the discovery of new spaces.

The different stages of research in altered gravity environments are all part of Dubois' process of creation and are integrated in the work itself. She relocates the limits of the body by taking risks – the rather abstract ones of dancers and the more practical ones of circus artist – and setting these in the space/time milieu of image and music.

Her aim is to give the audience the impression of weightlessness. Her choreography places the performers in states of "flight" – such as on trampoline - or spatial disorientation similar to those felt in zero gravity – to achieve an unsettling disorientation for the spectator, enhancing their imagination of their own bodies in a weightless state.

Kitsou Dubois, Jörg Müller, Matturin Bolze, Star City flight 2000
Video still: The Arts Catalyst

Kitsou Dubois, CNES flight
Video still: Ki Productions

Development of work

In the early 90s, Kitsou Dubois worked in collaboration with the French national space research centre (CNRS) where she developed a training programme for astronauts based on dance techniques. She participated in several parabolic flights with the French space agency (CNES), training and taking dancers into weightless conditions.

In 1998, she linked up with the Arts Catalyst and began a collaborative project with the Biodynamics Group, a team of scientists from a range of disciplines, from Imperial College of Science, Technology and Medicine, to investigate the control of movement in microgravity using insights from her own experiences of these conditions. The team submitted a successful proposal to the European Space Agency for participation on parabolic flight campaigns.

With the Imperial College Biodynamics Group, Kitsou Dubois participated as a co-investigator in the European Space Agency's 32nd and 34th parabolic flight campaigns in Bordeaux, France, on experiments in voluntary movement and posture (see section by Dr Nick Davey for scientific results).

Alongside this, she trained 3 other dancers - Mathurin Bolze, Jörg Müller and Laura de Nercy - for work in parabolic flight and in 2000 the company participated in a parabolic flight organised specifically for her research by Arts Catalyst and Projekt Atol Flight Operations at the Gagarin Cosmonaut Training Centre, Star City, Russia, in which she had the freedom to use most of the entire aircraft interior as a studio/stage for pure complex movement research during 10 parabolas.

During her work with Arts Catalyst, Dubois produced a 4-screen video installation Gravity Zero and a new film Fluid Trajectory analysing the work in parabolic flight. In 2002, both the Ballet

Kitsou Dubois, Gravity Zero 1999. Lux Centre, London
Photo: Andy Keate

Atlantique-Régine Chopinot in La Rochelle and La Maison de La Villette in Paris offered her residencies, which led to the creation of two works titled Fluid Trajectory, an installation and a performance for six artists. In the installation, made with collaborator Eric Duranteau, the way the dancers' movements are broken down in three dimensions is disturbing for the audience because the support points are no longer points of reference for our own position in relation to the performance.

The performance Fluid Trajectory is a multidisciplinary work, combining dance, acrobatics, juggling, images, music and visual arts. It uses all these elements for a single purpose: to propose tentative answers to the questions raised by the unique experience of weightlessness.

In the video installation File/Air, 2003, the third installation co-produced by Kitsou Dubois and Eric Duranteau, bodies glide endlessly and the eye and camera merge in a universe without landmarks. The "dance in an environment" developed by the choreographer is expressed here through the way the digital image is processed and set in space.

Kitsou Dubois continued her artistic career in the autumn of 2003 with the creation site Dancer, chair and shadow, in collaboration with the philosopher Roberto Casati.

In 2004, Kitsou Dubois developed a new project called Analogies, consisting in a series of laboratories including two parabolic flight campaigns in collaboration with the Space Observatory of the CNES/ Centre National d'Etudes Spatiales. This research process led to the creation of the Analogies performance for three dancers and three acrobats. It was created and performed in Parc de la Villette / Paris at the end of 2004.

List of works

Gravity Zero
performance, 1994
Credits
Choreography: Kitsou Dubois
Set Design: Goury
Music: Henry Torgues
Video Images: Jérôme de Missölz and Luc Riolon
Dancers: Lila Greene, Fabrice Guillot, Jörg Müller and Kitsou Dubois.
Performances
Théâtre Garonne, Toulouse
Théâtre des Malassis, Bagnolet
Parc de la Villette, Paris

Kitsou Dubois, a dancer in weightlessness
film, 1995
Credits
A film by Jérôme de Missölz, co-authored by Kitsou Dubois
Dancers: Lila Greene, Bertrand Lombard, Michèle Prelonge and Kitsou Dubois.
Screenings
Canal Plus

Gravity Zero
video installation 1999
Credits
Kitsou Dubois
Commissioned by The Arts Catalyst & the Lux Centre
Dancers: Lila Greene, Bertrand Lombard, Michèle Prelonge and Kitsou Dubois
Exhibitions
Lux Centre, London, UK (Arts Catalyst)
Museum für Gestaltung, Zurich

Fluid Trajectory
video 2001
Credits
Kitsou Dubois & Eric Duranteau
Commissioned by The Arts Catalyst
Dancers: Mathurin Bolze, Jörg Müller, Laura de Nercy and Kitsou Dubois
Zero G flight: Arts Catalyst & Projekt Atol Flight Operations
Screenings
Artists & Cosmonauts, Sadlers Wells, London, UK (Arts Catalyst)

Fluid Trajectory
video installation 2001
Credits
Kitsou Dubois & Eric Duranteau
Music: Alain Bellaïche
Dancers: Mathurin Bolze, Jörg Müller, Laura de Nercy and Kitsou Dubois
Zero G flight: Arts Catalyst & Projekt Atol Flight Operations
Exhibition
Creation: Event "Zero G" by Sampling, Paris
Presentation in La Rochelle Film Festival, Le Manege de Reims and the National Choreographic Center, le Havre.

Fluid Trajectory, performance 2002
Credits
Choreography: Kitsou Dubois
Set design: Goury
Images: Eric Duranteau
Music: Alain Bellaïche
Light design: Patrice Besombes
Dancers: Chloé Ban, Mathurin Bolze, Magali Caillet, Manu Debuck, Jörg Müller and Laura de Nercy
Zero G flight: Arts Catalyst & Projekt Atol Flight Operations
Performances
Centre Culturel Aragon, Tremblay en France
Maison de la Villette, Parc de la Villette
100 Dessus Dessous Festival, Parc de la Villette

File/Air
video installation 2003
Credits
Kitsou Dubois & Eric Duranteau
Music: Alain Bellaïche
Dancers: Mathurin Bolze, Jörg Müller, Laura de Nercy and Kitsou Dubois
Zero G flight: Arts Catalyst & Projekt Atol Flight Operations
Exhibition
@rt Outsiders Festival, La Maison Européenne de la Photographie, Paris, Monaco Dance Forum

The Dancer, the Chair and her Shadow
performance, 2003
Credits
Choreography: Kitsou Dubois
Set design: Goury
Light design: Patrice Besombes
Images: Eric Duranteau
Music: Alain Bellaïche
Scientific advise: Roberto Casati
Dancers: Chloé Ban, Francesca Bizzarri and Laura de Nercy
Exhibition
Centre Culturel Aragon, Tremblay en France

Analogies
performance, 2004
Credits
Choreography: Kitsou Dubois
Set design: Goury
Images: Eric Duranteau
Light design: Patrice Besombes
Music: Alain Bellaïche
Dancers: Chloé Ban, Manu Debuck, Xavier Kim, Bertrand Lombard, Chloé Moglia, Laura de Nercy
Zero G flight: Space Observatory/ CNES (Centre National d'Etudes Spatiales)
Exhibition
Maison de la Villette, Parc de la Villette, Paris
Le Manege de Reims
Forum Culturel du Blanc-Mesnil
Théâtre des Cordes, Centre Dramatique de Basse Normandie, Caen

Kitsou Dubois & Bertrand Lombard, CNES flight
Photos: Ki Productions

Mike Stubbs

Zero, video, 2001

Credits
Construction: Gina Czarnecki
Sound Design: Gerald Maire
Research commissioned by the Arts Catalyst.
Video commissioned by PVA MediaLab and Watershed Media Centre.
Flight: The Arts Catalyst & Projekt Atol Flight Operations
Distributed: LUX

Screenings
Micorwave, Hong Kong
Transmedialle, Berlin
Locative X, RIXC, Riga
Seafair, Skopje
Next 5 Minutes, Amsterdam
Biotech Era, Adelaide

Celebrating the 40th anniversary of Yuri Gagarin's first manned trip to space, in an age when space tourism has become a reality what does the future hold for our new born? A first shaft of light, a splinter of an image, first movements and a sense of independence. "Zero" is a lyrical view playing on the metaphor of weightlessness, mobility, existentialism and consciousness. At what point are we aware of our own bodies, what is private and where does the external world begin?

Using found footage and audio combined with super 8 film recorded by Mike Stubbs who was part of a team of artists and scientists invited onto a parabolic flight on a Russian military aircraft, based at the Yuri Gagarin Training Centre, Star City, Moscow, in 2000. The text comprises of writings by Net Robot, Netochka Nezvanova and poet Kevin Henderson. Read by Yuri Gagarin and Kevin Henderson.

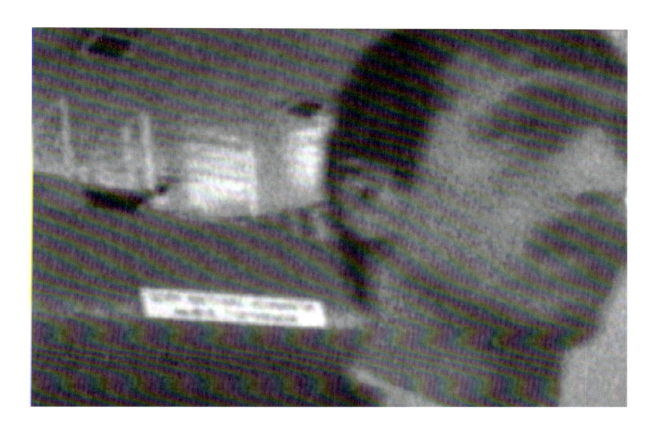

Mike Stubbs, Zero 2001
Video stills: Mike Stubbs

Ansuman Biswas and Jem Finer

wave/particle, video installation, 2001

Credits
Project commissioned by The Arts Catalyst
Flight: MIR Flight 001
Selected Screenings
Big Screen, Exchange Square, Manchester
Dartington Gallery, Devon
Artists and Cosmonauts, Sadlers Wells, London, UK (Arts Catalyst)
Planetary Bodies, Brighton

An installation in a sealed box, invisible to the eye, referring, like Schrödinger's famous cat, to the quantum mechanical uncertainty at the heart of the universe.

Alongside conceptual concerns were more practical questions. Musings on how interstellar travellers might exercise led to a consideration of swimming pools in space, and then a fascination with the complex behaviour of liquids in free fall. Wave/particle became an experiment. What would liquids do in microgravity?

Another challenge was to design a zero gravity musical instrument. While earth gongs and cymbals must vibrate around a fixed point, there is no such restriction in zero gravity. The Baoding Ball is an idiophone without a static fixing point. Dating back to Ming Dynasty China, it is now made in the same factories as aerospace products. The spheres chime as they float, and then are damped by acceleration against the walls, resulting in a sonification of the gravitational field.

A crate strapped to the aircraft floor was split into two. In one half a glass tank of water, sunflower oil, glycerine, and food dye sat on top of a light box. In the other, a padded box fitted with microphones, lights and a clear window, contained the balls. Video cameras recorded the contents.

The video is presented as a triptych, with a soundtrack derived from the chiming balls and aeroplane sounds. As colours and forms mutate and drift in the varying gravitational fields a harmony appears in the waves of liquid and ricocheting spheres.

Ansuman Biswas & Jem Finer, Wave/Particle 2001 (video still)

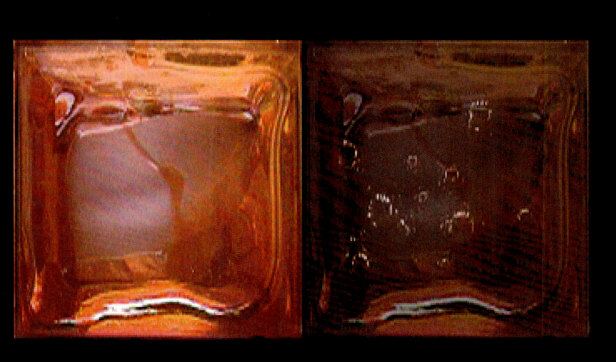

Ansuman Biswas and Jem Finer

zero genie, film, 2001

Credits
Project commissioned by The Arts Catalyst
Flight: MIR Flight 001
Selected Screenings:
Artists & Cosmonauts, Sadlers Wells, London, UK (Arts Catalyst)
Para-Site, Bridport Arts Centre, Dorset
Glastonbury Festival: short film tent
"Homeland", Exeter
Le Signal, Biarritz, France
Big Screen, ExchangeSquare, Manchester
Everything Normal, Cecil Sharp House, London, UK (Arts Catalyst)
Rencontres Internationales, Berlin
Dartington College of Arts, Devon
Blowing Up, London
Images Festival, Toronto, Canada
Rencontres Internationales, Paris
Kinofilm festival, Manchester
Tagawa International Short Film Festival, Japan
Crafting Space, Smart Project Space, Amsterdam
Exposures, London
Slightly Shady, London
Planetary Bodies, Brighton

On the surface, a playful attempt to perform feats ascribed to the genies and flying carpets of ancient myth, zero genie was conceived as a response to the structure and history of the space program over the last 50 years.

For millennia people have been travelling to the remotest regions of the cosmos using shamanistic technologies. Can we deride their experiences as being any less valid, any less real, than those of modern astronauts and cosmonauts? Who is to arbitrate on claims of yogic levitation, or persistent conspiracy theories suggesting that the American moon landings were actually a hoax constructed in a film studio? Judgements of fantasy and reality are conditioned by relationships of power. The vast expanse of space is a political territory, colonised so far by the industrialized, affluent powers. Its exploration is a First World, high investment pursuit, beyond the orbit of all but the whitest, richest individuals.

Ansuman Biswas and Jem Finer, dressed in turbans, jewelled waistcoats, baggy pyjamas and curly toed sandals present a foil to the military industrial complex. In the belly of a plunging Soviet troop carrier, they attempt to smoke a pipe together, play shawms, dance, and ride the mythical flying carpet.

The resulting ten-minute film is simultaneously magical and hilarious. It has been shown to great acclaim in many venues around the world.

Ansuman Biswas & Jem Finer, Zero Genie 2001
Photo: GCTC/The Arts Catalyst

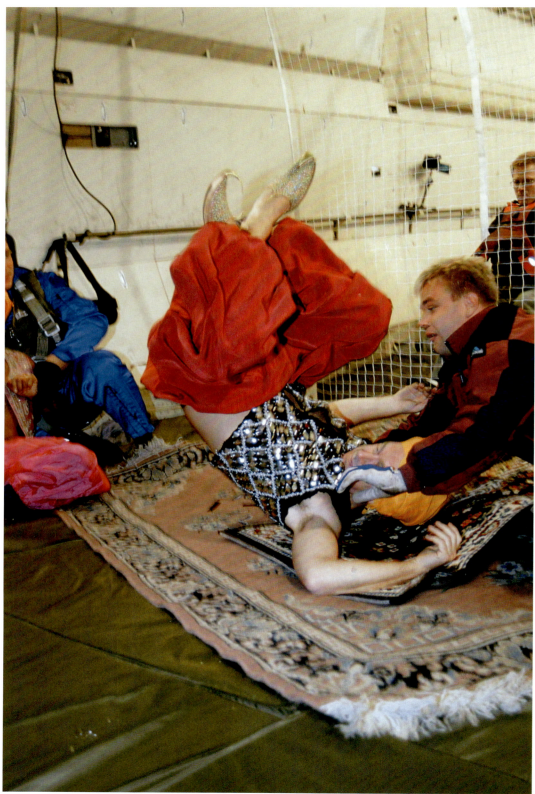

Ansuman Biswas & Jem Finer, Zero Genie 2001
Photo: GCTC/The Arts Catalyst

Zero Genies perform,
Cosmonauts Club, Star City
Photo: Alexander Volokhovsky

Andrew Kötting

Too G, film, 2001

Credits
Film made by Andrew Kötting.
Project commissioned by The Arts Catalyst
Flight: MIR Flight 001
Screenings/Exhibitions
Artists & Cosmonauts, Sadlers Wells, London, UK (Arts Catalyst)
MIR Microgravity Seminar, V2_Institute for the Unstable Media, Rotterdam, The Netherlands (V2/MIR)
MIR: Art in Variable Gravity, Cornerhouse, Manchester, UK (Arts Catalyst/MIR)
Everything Normal, Cecil Sharp House, London, UK (Arts Catalyst)

"Everything normal. Everything working perfectly."

Andrew Kötting's video 'Too G' was made after Arts Catalyst's second trip to the Gagarin Centre in 2001.

Inspired by the overwhelming force of 2G and the ensuing befuddlement, the work might be read as a tongue-in-cheek homage to Yuri Gagarin, the people of Star City and the pioneering artists who attempted to create work on a plunging aircraft. Kötting provides an insight into the madness of experimentation in the extreme environment of a zero gravity flight on a Russian military base, where Gagarin's face smiles down at you from almost every building.

A wobbly B-film rocket follows a similar trajectory to the parabolic flight path, reaching for the stars before plummeting nose cone first back into the hard Earth, echoing the Russian's more brutal approach to re-entry landings than the NASA ocean splashdowns. The rocket's flight links a kaleidoscope of grainy archive images from Moscow, Star City and the parabolic flight on which Kötting participated.

Left: Andrew Kötting, Too G 2001 (video still)
Right: Andrew Kötting with brain
Photo: The Arts Catalyst

Morag Wightman

Falling without Fear, performance in zero-g, 2001
Gravity – a love story, 25' performance, 2002

Credits
Artistic director: Morag Wightman
Performer (zero-G): Morag Wightman
Set & costumes (zero-g & ground): Helga Goellner
3-screen video projection work: Gavin Lockhart
Performers (ground): Veronica Forioso, Steven Whinnery, Graham Clint
Soundtrack: Little Japanese Toy, Amir Shoat & Iain Ross
Rigging: Will Harding
Commissioned by The Arts Catalyst
Flight: MIR Flight 001
Performance
Artsits & Cosmonauts, Sadlers Wells, London, UK (Arts Catalyst)
Water movement, film & dance research:
Chisenhale Dance Space, London
Screening
ArtSci2002, The CUNY Graduate Center, New York

Morag Wightman's solo performance Falling without Fear onboard a parabolic flight evolved from her need to intellectually and artistically explore the concept of 'suspension' in an environment where fear of falling is not an issue. As an aerial artist, each ground-based performance poses a challenge: to perform at great height while appearing carefree.

Falling without Fear spanned 7 parabolas. During the first two parabolas, Morag Wightman attached the long rope to her harness and, inverting the rules of suspension, rose towards the ceiling held back on her flight only by the tug of the rope. At the onset of the third parabola, she released the rope to indicate a transition from suspension to flight.

The brief encounter with weightlessness revealed gravity to Morag Wightman in a new way. She recognised the love-hate relationship that binds humans permanently to gravity, while weightlessness taunts as an apparently ideal environment. Her performance work Gravity – a love story tackles this problematic relationship in a humorous way. A specially designed suspension system enables a semblance of flight. Suspended skiers slide across slopes of air and frolic in their aerial medium with backflips and somersaults. These scenes alternate with sequences emphasising inertia and weight. Into this exposition of gravity she introduces a 3-screen projection of images from microgravity for a visual interplay between immediate and remembered space.

Morag Wightman, Falling without Fear 2001
Photo: Nicola Triscott

Morag Wightman, Falling without Fear 2001
Photo: Nicola Triscott

Morag Wightman, Falling without Fear
2001
Photo: Nicola Triscott

Anthony Bull, Louise K Wilson, Morag Wightman

A preliminary study of different movement control techniques utilised by a dancer (Morag) and non-dancer (Louise) in microgravity conditions. This was undertaken by Dr Anthony Bull, a bioengineering researcher at Imperial College London, Department of Bioengineering, in collaboration with the two artists on MIR Flight 001, Art Catalyst's zero gravity 'parabolic' flight from the Gagarin Cosmonaut Training Centre, Star City, Russia. This work has extended into a dialogue on many levels between the 3 researchers.

Interdisciplinary Microgravity Movement Research: Experiments on a Zero Gravity Flight, 2001

Credits
Research supported by The Arts Catalyst
Flight: MIR Flight 001
Presentations
Artists & Cosmonauts, Sadlers Wells, London, UK (Arts Catalyst)
ArtSci2002, The CUNY Graduate Center, New York US

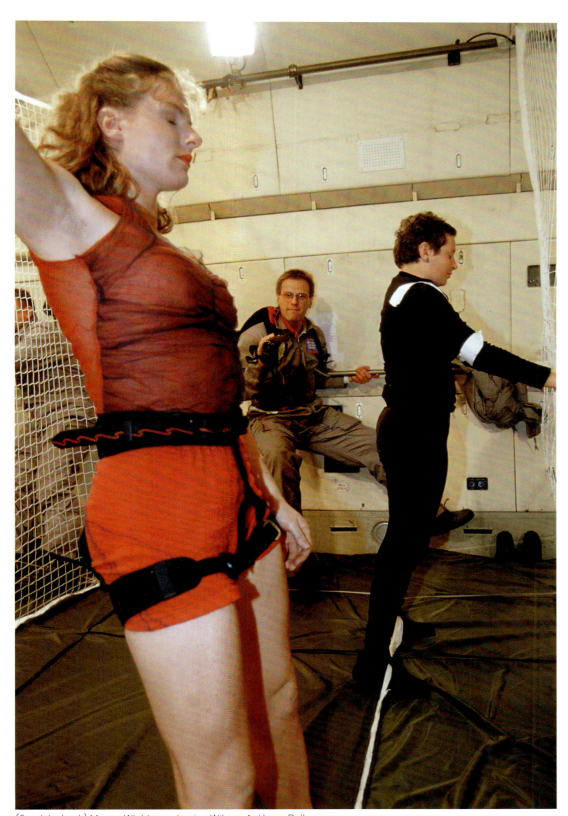

(front to back) Morag Wightman, Louise Wilson, Anthony Bull
Photo: Nicola Triscott

Flow Motion
Edward George, Anna Piva, Trevor Mattison

Kosmos in Blue, workshop & live performance, 2001

Credits:
Sound & images: Edward George, Anna Piva, Trevor Mattison
Commissioned by The Arts Catalyst
Flight: MIR Flight 001
Performances
Cosmonauts Club, Star City, Russia
Artists & Cosmonauts, Sadlers Wells, London, UK (Arts Catalyst)
Cosmonauts (The Arts Catalyst)

Flow Motion perform Kosmos in Blue, Star City, 2001
Photo: The Arts Catalyst

Kosmos In Blue was a 3-part work comprising participation on the Arts Catalyst's zero gravity workshop in parabolic flight at the Gagarin Cosmonaut Training Centre in Star City, a live performance of Hallucinator material at the Cosmonauts' Club, mixing the sounds of radio astronomy with remixes of Sun Ra material, and a CD of this material plus material gathered during the trip to Star City.

With Kosmos In Blue, Flow Motion was concerned with questions of troubled subjectivity, of isolation and freedom, of melancholia; the focal figure was Sun Ra.

Sun Ra was without a doubt 20th century American music's most consistent, significant advocate of a star-bound earth-based music. His heliocentric vision was rooted in a sense of unbelonging here on earth, a wistful, romantic but nonetheless very real sense of displacement; a kind of heightened, profound loneliness. Ra's music always seemed to be aimed at, or searching for, potential fellow travellers, possible cosmonauts, disaffected earth dwellers, profoundly constrained by the lack of space – physical, political, existential, spiritual – here in their own home.

Andrey & Julia Velikanov

Universal Substitute, video, 2001

Credits
Music by Flow Motion, London
'Tenderness' (music by Alexandra Pakhmutova, lyrics by Grebennikov and N. Dobronravov) performed by Rob La Frenais
English by Joseph Schoen
Made in association with The Art Catalyst, London
Flight: MIR Flight 001
Screenings
TV Gallery, Moscow
Artists & Cosmonauts, Sadlers Wells, London, UK (Arts Catalyst)

Shot on October 3, 2001 at the Cosmonauts Training Centre in Zvezdny.

Materials used:

videos on Russian and American space research programs

fragments from Tatiana Lioznova's 'Three Poplars in Pluschikha'

Renny Harlin's 'Die Hard 2'

Wolfgang Petersen's 'Air Force One'

fragments of coverage of tragic events in September and October 2001:

September 11 - terror attacks on New York and Washington

October 4 - Ukrainian S-200 missile destroys a Russian civilian airplane over the Black sea

October 7 - cities in Afghanistan attacked from the air

October 8 - nuclear submarine "Kursk" elevated from the bottom of the Barents sea

October 15 - anthrax panic in the US

Left: Ansuman Biswas
Right: Cosmonauts Museum, Star City
Photos: The Arts Catalyst

Nick J Davey and team (Imperial College Biodynamics Group/ Ki Productions/ Arts Catalyst)

Voluntary movement and posture in zero gravity

Credits
Research supported by The Arts Catalyst
Flight: MIR Flight 001
Presentations
Artists & Cosmonauts, Sadlers Wells, London, UK (Arts Catalyst)
Cosmonauts (The Arts Catalyst)
ArtSci2002, The CUNY Graduate Center, New York

The team: Nick Davey, Steve Rawlinson, Alex Nowicky, Bob Schroter, Alison McGregor and Paul Strutton (Imperial College London), Kitsou Dubois, Matturin Bolze (Ki Productions), Nicola Triscott and Rob La Frenais (The Arts Catalyst)

In an unusual interdisciplinary research collaboration, Imperial College's Biodynamics Group - a team of scientists from a range of disciplines, has been working with French choreographer and movement researcher Dr Kitsou Dubois to investigate the control of movement in weightlessness. Specifically, the team has set out to investigate how the nervous system controls the subtle process of adjusting posture. And whether people who are very good at moving their bodies, like dancers, have a better-developed control system.

In this first investigation, led by neuroscientist Dr Nick Davey, the team wished to find out how it is that the back muscles contract to counter arm movements on the opposite side. Is this controlled by the brain in a coordinated way – does the brain switch on the pathways to the left back at the same time as those to the right arm? Or is it a reflex response? The team measured how active different muscles were at different times by recording electricity or electromyography (EMG) produced by the muscles, and how active the pathway from the brain was, for which transcranial magnetic stimulation (TMS) was used. With TMS, magnetic pulses stimulate those nerves in the brain that project to back muscles, enabling the team to investigate how the responses in the back muscles to TMS change when the arm is extended.

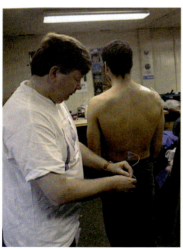

Left: Nick Davey attaches muscle recording electrodes to the back of dancer Matturin Bolze, acting as experimental subject
Right: Steve Rawlinson and Kitsou Dubois discuss the experimental procedure
Photos: Imperial College Biodynamics Group

Gravity's action on the body brings into play balance organs in the ear as well as touch and stretch sensitive organs in the skin, joints and muscles, which can confuse the results, so the team wished to perform the experiment in zero gravity. The team applied to and was accepted for participation in the European Space Agency's 32nd and 34th ESA parabolic campaigns in 2002 and 2003.

They found, both on the ground and in zero gravity, that the back muscles were turned on when the arm was extended and that the pathways from the voluntary control areas of the brain were more active when this happened. This told them, overall, that the drive to the back muscles is stronger when the opposite arm is extended and that it is the brain's voluntary control areas that control the stabilisation mechanism. The team concluded that the sense organs in the skin, joints and muscles were not heavily involved and that the stabilisation of the body during arm extension was not simply a reflex response.

Another interesting result was the response of the body's muscle to removing gravity. Rather than relaxing in weightlessness, as one might expect, the muscles of the back in fact became more active regardless of the position of the opposite arm. In other words the spine became more inflexible in zero gravity rather than the more flexible state it is in on the ground. The team thinks that this process enables the body to orientate itself more easily when its gravitational point of reference is removed.

Left: Transcranial magnetic stimulation (TMS) being applied to the brain of Alison McGregor, acting as experimental subject
Photo: Imperial College Biodynamics Group
Right: The Novespace A300 Airbus climbing at the precise angle of 47 degrees before a period of zero gravity
Photo: European Space Agency

Marcel.li Antúnez Roca

Dédalus Project, microperformances, 2003
Transpermia, lecture-performance, 2003

Credits
Concept, writing, drawings & performer: Marcel.lí Antúnez Roca:
Music: Alain Wergifosse
Programmer: Jesus de la Calle
Head technician, Flight technician, Sound & lights: Paco Beltrán,
Flash animation, Flight technician: Álvaro Uña
Flash animation: Gaetano Mangano
Typography: Carlos Romera
Video editor: Sergi Díez
Costumes: Júlia Rubio
Flight & ground camera: Begoña Egurbide
Flight camera: Saso Podgorsek
Flight choreographer: Boris Naidyonov (Gagarin Cosmonaut Training Centre)
Produced by Panspermia S.L. and Arts Catalyst/MIR Project
Producer & management: Marta Oliveres
Flight: MIR Campaign 2003
Commissioned by The Arts Catalyst and the MIR Consortium (Arts Catalyst, Projekt Atol, V2, Leonardo Olats, Multimedia Complex for Actual Arts)

Performances
MIR Microgravity Seminar, Shouwburg Theatre, Rotterdam, The Netherlands (V2/MIR)
Extremophiles, Royal Institution of Great Britain, London, UK (Arts Catalyst/MIR)
@rt Outsiders Festival, Maison de la Photographie, Paris, France

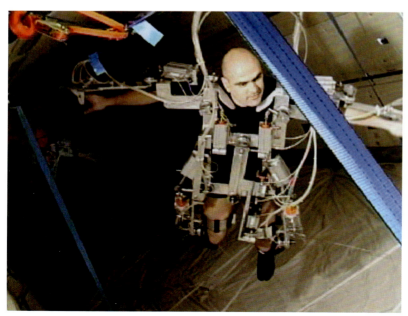

Marcel.li Antúnez Roca, Dédalus Project 2003
Video still: The Arts Catalyst/Panspermia

The Dédalus Project consisted of a series of 25 zero gravity microperformances, taking place in 25 parabolas over two flights.

The microperformances were organised around two devices: the Réquiem bodybot (a wearable robot that controls the body) and the dresskeleton (an exoskeleton that enables interaction between the movements of the body and projected films and robots).

Taken as an experiment, the microperformances had varying results. On the six parabolas during which the artist was inside Réquiem and moved by its pneumatic sequences, the foreseen paradoxical floatability was not achieved, due to the caution of the flight controllers in releasing the securing ropes, so that instead of becoming a metaphor for lightness, the experiment became the paradox of control. The nineteen parabolas of the dresskeleton interface were more satisfactory. The oscillation of the range sensors on the dresskeleton produced by the movements of elbows, shoulder blades and knees in weightlessness activated the films and the softbot (zero-g robot). Three interactive films were prepared for this experiment with different graphic contents based on three subjects: microbiology, transgenics and bio-robots.

This experiment led the artist to his first reflections on the absence of gravity. As he has gone deeper into the results, his interests have extended to other aspects of human space exploration.

Scientists say that certain remains (stromatolites) show that life originated on earth more than six hundred million years ago, but the mechanism that gave rise to it is unknown. Amongst the different hypotheses is the Panspermia theory. This theory suggests that asteroids with biological material crashed into the earth, giving rise to life. From this assumption, it could be said that the evolution of life, is returning, after two million years, to where it came from: space. This could be termed inverse Panspermia – that is, Transpermia.

The conquest of space is one of the most extensive and complex challenges of our time. The exosphere is agravic, anaerobic and radioactive, that is, extremophilous for humans. And to inhabit it, an entirely new world must be redesigned. In space, artifice and nature merge. It as the place where everything is conceivable, everything is possible, everything remains to be done. This Transpermia is the space for utopia. For Roca, his prototypes, such as robots, corporal interfaces and systemic software, find a new frame of definition in Transpermia.

Marcel.lí Antúnez Roca, Dédalus Project 2003
Video still: The Arts Catalyst/Panspermia

Left: Marcel.lí Antúnez Roca with Pol exoskeleton
Photo: Panspermia
Right: Marcel.lí Antúnez Roca, Dédalus Project 2003
Video still: The Arts Catalyst/Panspermia